Your Baby

& Your Work

Your Baby
& Your Work

Balancing Your Life

A National Childbirth Trust Guide

Teresa Wilson

FISHER
er
BOOKS™

Publishers:	Howard W. Fisher Bill Fisher Helen V. Fisher	**Illustrations:**	Mike Edwards Pete Welford Jo Dennis

Managing Editor: Sarah Trotta

**North American
  Editor:** Margaret Martin

Production: Deanie Wood
Randy Schultz

Cover Design: FifthStreet*design*,
Berkeley, CA

Cover Photo: Zefa/Ronnie
Kaufman

Photo Credits:
The publishers would like to thank the following for their permission to reproduce photographs: Michael Bassett: pages xii, 30, 92, 104, 126; David Muscroft: page 20; Julian Cotton Photo Library: page 46; The Image Bank/M. Regine: page 58; The Image Bank/Romilly Lockyer: page 76; Graham Bell: page 134; Egnell Ameda: page 146.

Published by
Fisher Books
4239 W. Ina Road, Suite 101
Tucson, Arizona 85741
(520) 744-6110

First published in Great Britain in 1996 as *Work and Home: Finding the Balance* © 1996 NCT Publishing Ltd. North American edition
© 1997 Fisher Books

**Library of Congress
Cataloging-in-Publication Data**

Wilson, Teresa.
  [Work and Home]
  Your baby and your work / Teresa Wilson.
      p. cm. — (A National Childbirth Trust guide)
  Originally published under title: Work and Home. London : HMSO in association with the National Childbirth Trust, 1996.
    Includes index.
    ISBN 1-55561-126-5
    1. Working mothers—Great Britain.
2. Work and Family—Great Britain. I. Title. II. Series.
    HQ759.48.W56 1997
    306.874'3—DC21   97-22975
                                              CIP

Printed in U.S.A.
Printing 5 4 3 2

Contents

About the Author

Teresa Wilson has tried all kinds of ways to work and run a family. She has been a full-time, stay-at-home mother. She has worked part-time. And she has worked full-time. Over the years she has learned that each has its own benefits and problems. She thinks it is important to accept that your life will always be changing once you have had children. Different ways of working will suit different stages in your life as a family.

She has three children, ages 15, 5 and 2. She is a breastfeeding counselor and trainee postnatal-discussion leader for the National Childbirth Trust (NCT). She also works as an editor for *New Generation,* the journal of the NCT.

Publisher's Note

All comments and personal accounts were given to us in confidence. Out of respect for our contributors' privacy we have changed all names.

We have tried where possible to reproduce quotations verbatim. Where editing has been applied, the meaning of the quotation has been maintained.

Acknowledgments

—are numerous. First, a large thank-you to my family, who tolerated my working the most antisocial hours for six months and cleared up the mess after me. Special thanks are due to my husband, Rick, who spent many lonely evenings, and acted as a single parent most weekends. Thanks are due, too, to my dear mom, Pat, who did all she could to ease the load, so I could work. Anyone who wonders if they can work from home with children around—take it from me—you can't! So without their support, this book would not have been written.

Thanks also to Vanessa Von Pralitz and Alison Howarth-Jarrett, who supported me with childcare on short notice and to Jenny Jolliffe for reading and checking the manuscript.

Many thanks also to the working parents who gave up their precious time to talk with me. I know it wasn't always easy to give it. But they wanted to talk about the pleasures and pitfalls of their lifestyle. And they wanted to pass on things they wish they had known in advance.

Finally, thank you to my editor, Daphne Metland, whose firm direction supported me along the way.

This book is dedicated to my children: Mat, Sean and Alex.

Introduction

This book aims to give a broad view of how women combine raising their children and working.

There are important choices to be made. Should you go back to work at all? Should you choose a new way of working? And what sort of childcare will be best? Your choice will also depend on how old your child is when you return. Then, when you think life is getting simpler, along comes school to throw off your plans. How do you cope with all those vacation days?

A working family also brings into sharper relief the pressures of work. There is often a lack of time for leisure pursuits and enjoying the children. For couples, there may be discussion on how best to work together and share the parenting role. For single parents, there are issues of parenting alone and where to find support.

One thing is always true. There is never enough time for everything. If you have a whole day at work, you still have to do the chores for that day, and give your child your full attention.

Most parents can combine working and parenting. But it can be stressful. And it can be tiring. On a good day you may feel satisfied that you have achieved a new dimension to your life. But the balance between your job and your family can be hard to maintain. There may be times when you need to place a greater focus on one or the other.

I spoke with many working parents while researching this book. I believe their views reflect society in general and the questions raised about being a working parent.

I have aimed to reflect the many ways of working that now exist and the kinds of childcare you can choose. But each parent I spoke with said the same thing: No matter what, it is never easy to decide to return to work after you have had a child.

Chapter 1

Why Do Women Return to Work?

The Big Picture

The issue of whether to return to work or not after starting a family used to be more clear-cut. Families were started earlier, often soon after marriage. For many women the question of work was not even raised. For others, starting a family meant that you didn't intend to work, at least until your children had left home. After that, you might start to do volunteer work or take a part-time, nondemanding job. And for some women there was no question of having children, because it would interfere with their career.

Women today can combine a working life with a family. It is starting to get easier. There has been a slow but steady increase in childcare options. No longer do women have to choose between returning to work full-time or risk losing their jobs. Employers, encouraged by new laws, have begun to show a flexible attitude to their female employees.

Guilt

It's worth getting this word out in the open right away. When we look at why women want to return to work, a cloud gathers that spells out the word "guilt." Some women are still told that they should feel guilty about leaving their child to pursue a career. Others feel guilty about *not* feeling guilty when they leave their child. It is a personal issue. No doubt many women do suffer from strong guilt feelings about returning to work. Some come to terms with it because they know they cannot afford to stay home. Others feel guilty until they know that their child is happy in childcare.

BACKGROUND NOTES

Your Maternity Rights

Working pregnant women have certain legal rights to protect their health and, in some cases, their job. It's worth checking these, as they tend to be complex. Laws and benefits in the United States differ a great deal from those in Canada. They also change from time to time. The main benefits are:

United States' Family and Medical Leave Act

You are covered if:

- your company employs 50 or more workers.
- you have worked at least 1,250 hours in the past 12 months.

Companies with fewer than 50 workers are not required to extend maternity leave.

Benefits include:

- up to 12 weeks of unpaid leave. This can be taken all at once, or by reducing hours, if you agree. But you have to give 30 days' notice.

You will retain your health benefits while you are on leave, but you must pay for them yourself.

Other restrictions may apply. Some states have laws that may provide added benefits.

You may want to consult a lawyer who specializes in employment law.

Workers in the United States who do not qualify have no legal right to any maternity leave. Such workers may use sick leave, if they have some. Or they may negotiate a leave with their employer. But they have no legal right to a leave, or to retain their job, if their employer decides to replace them.

Canadian Maternity and Parental Benefits

If you qualify, you may receive employment insurance benefits if you are:

- pregnant;
- adopting a child;
- caring for a newborn baby.

Maternity benefits may only be paid to the natural mother of a child. Parental benefits may be paid to both natural and adoptive parents. Benefits do not increase if you have a multiple birth or adopt more than one child.

To qualify for maternity or parental benefits, you must have worked at least 700 hours in the past 52 weeks.

How much you will receive:

Most people will receive 55% of their normal incomes. Those with low incomes and dependents may receive up to 65% in 1997. This amount will increase each year until 2002. The first check will be received by the end of the fourth week after you apply for benefits.

Maternity Benefits

Maternity benefits can be taken for up to 15 weeks. They can be taken both before and after the birth of a child. But unless a baby is confined to a hospital, they can't be received later than 17 weeks after a baby is due, or born.

Parental Benefits

Parental benefits can be taken for up to 10 weeks. They may be taken by both natural or adoptive parents. Benefits may be claimed by one parent or split between two.

How to apply:

Contact your nearest Human Resource Centre of Canada (HRCC). You will need:

- your Social Insurance Number (SIN);
- your Record of Employment (ROE). This is a form your employer must give you. It tells how long you worked and how much you earned with that employer. If you have worked for more than one employer in the last 52 weeks, you may have more than one ROE.

* adoption certificate for adoptive parents who apply for parental benefits.

Your Rights

Maternity rights have improved. As more and more women use these rights, things can only get better. To learn about the laws that affect your rights in your state, contact the Women's Bureau of the United States Department of Labor (see Resources). In Canada, contact your nearest Human Resource Centre of Canada (HRCC).

Conditions are getting better in the United States and Canada. But there is still a long way to go before we reach the standards set by Sweden.

SWEDISH RIGHTS

Since the early 1970s, Sweden has had a policy and benefits aimed at helping parents, not just mothers, remain at work while caring for children. In Sweden, employment benefits include:

• Pregnancy leave of 50 days

• Paternity leave of 10 days

• Parental leave (to care for young children or babies) of 12 months per child. Leave of 90 days per year per child under 12 to care for them if sick or if their caregiver is sick.

All these are paid state benefits at 80% to 100% of earnings.

Reasons for Returning

Loneliness of Motherhood

Loneliness is one of the toughest issues mothers face when they have their first child.

Very often they haven't worked near home, so they don't know the neighbors very well. People who go off for the day to work and those who stay at home lead different lives. It takes a while to adjust. A working woman will have been in control of her life in a different way. She is able to make decisions and act upon them right away. The arrival of a child can frustrate her for a while. There is no one to turn to at this stage. No wonder people yearn to go back to the warmth and friendliness of a working life!

Patty explains: *"Sam was born in November. The clocks had rolled back. It was dark by four. I can remember that horrible time between four and six, waiting for Simon to come home. I was desperate for him to come through the door, so I could hand Sam over to him. Since I had worked in the city, I didn't know many people nearby. And I didn't know anyone with babies. You don't have time, and it takes a while to build up contacts. Before you have children, your network is at the office.*

I was also very cautious about going out with the stroller in snow and ice. All this made me feel very cooped up."

Louisa felt the same way: *"After your first baby, there is no social sphere. It's one endless day. And you're not used to having an endless day. There's only so much shopping you can do."*

If you feel lonely, what steps can you take?

It can take a long time to build up a new set of contacts and friends when you have a baby. Even though you may go back to work in three months, it can be worthwhile getting to know local people with babies and young children. It's nice to get together with these people and their children on weekends.

You may miss your baby when you are at work. You might wonder what he is doing during the week and who he is meeting.

REASONS TO WORK

- Need to earn money for the household
- Emotional need to work
- Intellectual need to work
- Single parenthood
- Planning for the future— pensions and security
- Staying involved
- Maintaining an established career
- Benefiting your children
- A sense of your own value
- Better childcare
- Childhood influences

A Need for More Than Just Babies ...

Amy had the same views as her husband: *"We wanted to have an equal, sharing partnership. Neither of us liked the thought of me being the only one to take care of the household. My first baby was 14 months old when my second baby was born. I'm sure I would have found having two babies for company all day very frustrating."*

Some women feel that being at home with the baby would not stretch them enough intellectually. They feel they become better mothers when they keep their minds engaged.

Beth feels this way. She is the mother of five children. She feels strongly

WHERE TO MEET OTHER PEOPLE

- Your baby clinic
- Postpartum discussion or fitness classes
- La Leche League meetings
- Baby swim classes
- Baby gym classes
- Local women's group

that both she and the children benefit by her working: *"If I'm not working, then I start mentally climbing walls. I need to use my mind. That's just the kind of person I am!"*

Do the Children Benefit?

The idea that work can give a mother more to give back to her children is a common feeling.

"I think I would be a worse mother, being home all day. If you aren't with the children all the time, you enjoy seeing them more when you are together. You enjoy doing things with them, too."

"I know that my kids like me working. I am a better mother if I am fulfilled. I can also use my work as a tool when I am with my children. For example, I just learned American Sign Language. I can talk to my children about it and share it. As a teacher, we all enjoy doing homework together. It becomes a really good time."

Kerry also felt a need to use her brain at work: *"I didn't know many neighbors before having Jo. All the neighbors we do know, we know because of Jo. The thing we have in common is the children. That's what we talk about, which is fine. But I also really enjoy the chance to talk to other people about other things. I like working with people. I like managing people. That's what I value work for: the chance to use my brain."*

A Secure Future

Today, many women want to be in control of their own lives. With the divorce rate high, there is a greater need to protect your financial future.

Even without taking a career break, retirement payments may not work as well for women as they do for men. Women live longer. They have to put more into their retirement plan to get the same-size payments out. That's because it has to last those extra years.

During a career break you may not be able to pay into a retirement plan. Women who are looking at their own financial future may not want to give up five years, or so, of payments toward their retirement. They will need more to benefit from in later years. But there may be tax-deferred ways around the problem. Tax laws can change, also. You may want to consult a tax or pension specialist.

Sue learned from her parents' separation that nothing is set in stone: *"My parents split up. I need to know I can cope if something like that happens to me. It's important to me to feel secure. I need a degree of independence. Although I'm married to Alan, I need to know that if something happened, I could cope."*

When you have children for whom you must provide, you may begin to feel more responsible. Providing for children is no longer seen as solely the male responsibility. It's not just divorce that is considered here. Sometimes partners die young. The unspeakable does happen. And some women make moves to protect their family's finances.

Staying Involved

Many aspects of work life can change quickly. In order to keep your job, you have to keep your job skills current.

Rita, for example, is a scientist: *"Things move very fast. I have to stay involved with the profession in order to keep up with it."*

Some companies permit career breaks. But you may have to go in at least for at least two weeks a year, to keep up and update work skills. This is nearly always the case if you use computers in your working life.

Sue is an accountant: *"In this career you'd be out of date if you left it for a couple of years. Also, I'm not a very confident person. I can't bluff my way into a job. I need to know that my knowledge is thorough."*

Being seen at work, rather than having the message filter through that you are doing mothering now, can improve your own self-esteem at work. It can seem easy to feel written off if you're not around the office for a few months. And what happens when you come back? There's no doubt that it can be harder to find the right niche if you have to push your way back into the market a couple of years later with rusty skills.

There are other reasons too why you might need to stay where you are. Frances is blind. *"If I were sighted, I wouldn't feel I needed to keep the job open in the same way. But it was much harder for me to get a job when I finished college than for any of my friends. I can't give it up now."*

Maintaining a Career and Way of Life

Having a baby *after* a career has become established means there is more to lose by giving up work and staying at home with the baby.

As Jillian says, *"I worked so hard to get where I am now. I don't want to give it up."*

Some women believe that you don't have to give up anything. The Superwoman idea still prevails. Childless couples tend to socialize with other childless friends. And families have greater mobility. As a result, a childless or pregnant woman has fewer chances to see just how much time and effort a baby takes. There is no opportunity to see how a baby will change things, or the way that you feel.

Patty says, *"You think life is going to be the same. You have no idea how it will really change your life. If you have a career, you don't want to miss out."*

A Financial Need

Many, many people have to go back to work after having a baby. They work because living is very expensive now. Carolyn had to return to work sooner than she wanted because she and her husband couldn't manage without the extra income: *"I wanted to get by until Tom was in school. But he was only 3 years old when business problems got us into debt. Going back to work was the only option. I had to do it. The funny thing is that, now I've started work, I need it. It woke up my brain. I wouldn't be happy walking to school and back any more. I do miss part of it . . . our talks . . . but I wouldn't want to stop work."*

Layoffs are a fact of life for many people. Some years ago it was possible to believe that you had a job for life, unless disaster befell you or the company. Today layoffs are common.

For Joan, her husband's layoff meant, among other things, a lot of resentment: *"When Peter lost his job my feeling was, and still is, that it isn't fair. We waited a long time before having our family. We wanted to be financially secure. I planned to stay at home and look after them. Now I have to work, just to keep the bills paid. And we still can't afford any extras."*

Your Own Childhood

Our own mothers are often our first role model. What they did when we were children can affect what we do ourselves. *"Because my mother worked, we had nannies. There were four of us—all girls. We had a very happy childhood and the nannies became part of the family. In fact, the last one is still living with my parents. I've followed in my mother's footsteps. My children are looked after by a live-in nanny."*

But some daughters prefer the complete opposite of what their mother did, like Sue: *"My mother was always there with me. She never left me to play. So I was a very clingy child. I think a lot of that was due to not mixing very much, and being with my mother most of the time. I wouldn't want my daughter to be as dependent on me as I was on my mother. So I've gone back to work part-time."*

Gina's own childhood had the opposite effect on her: *"I was born in South America. We had servants, including a nanny. But when I was 7 and my sister was 5, we were sent to boarding school. We were told there were no decent schools where we were. I hated it. I wrote to my parents all the time to let me come home. We only saw our parents once a year, during summer vacations. Our grandparents lived near our school so we weren't all alone. But that didn't help much."* Gina feels this experience has a lot to do with why she started a family childcare center, rather than going back to work. She can stay with her own children while she provides care for others.

Lindsay wanted to work. But she also wanted to be with her children. So she took on work she could do from home: *"Above all, I wanted to be there for my children. My mother was there for me throughout my childhood. But I also thought it was important for me to use my brain. Working from home seems to provide the answer so far."*

Kerry found her parents were a very useful role model. They combined working with bringing up children. *"Having working parents makes you aware that you can have two working adults in the family and things work out."*

Single Parenting

Being a single parent is likely to restrict the number of choices you have, unless you are financially secure. If there is only you, there is only one income. You will need to look at the balance between income and payments for childcare and living expenses. You may need to improve your job skills to earn enough to get by. And you may have to double up and share an apartment or house. But you may be able to receive some support while you complete a job-training program. Some programs offer single parents help in finding secure employment.

Single parents often feel lonely. If you are at home with the children, and your partner comes home, you can hand over your children for a while, at least, and take a break. You also have someone to let off steam to. Your partner can listen to you talking in detail about the color of the baby's dirty diapers that day. You can tell your partner about the number

of gurgles she made, or how you are sure that she's starting to smile at you.

If you are on your own, you don't have those opportunities. You have to figure out by yourself how to take the breaks you need. There may be other people you can talk to about your baby's growth, but not all the time. Even though babies are very lovable and you may want to talk about them, single parenting can be a grind. Single parents have few chances to be an adult with another person.

Having a job to go to could, therefore, be more important if you are not sharing your life with another adult. It means that you can function on two levels, rather than just being involved with children. It gives a social outlet and a sense of independence.

It is also worth looking at from the point of view of the children. The children may benefit from having different adults caring for them during the day. They may learn how to relate to other people besides their parent.

A Sense of Your Own Value

Being a parent changes your view of the world and where you fit in. In some places you are accepted and respected. In others you might find people are reserved. You might even find that people resent or envy you.

When you consider whether to return to work or not you may feel weighed down by decisions. It doesn't help to have an employer who isn't supportive. You may begin to feel that there is little chance of being able to get what you want.

Alex is a marketing director. But when she became pregnant for the first time, she was a marketing manager: *"It is very important to bargain for what you want. When you are in the job, your position is stronger. Of course you will be told 'we don't do that here.' But there's a first time for everything!*

"I think women often don't value themselves enough. They think they have to take what is offered because they are lucky to have a job. But if they are doing that job well, the company won't want to lose them. They have spent money training them. They are an asset to the company. It's worth thinking about this when you ask for conditions that suit your needs."

There are so many more working mothers now that it should be possible to find jobs that work well for your family. Mothers who work part-time tend to work harder than before to justify their shortened hours. Most companies won't lose anything, but will gain loyal members of their workforce.

Work and Lifestyles

Women are learning to adapt work to suit their life. They no longer sacrifice all their personal goals for "the job." Children and their needs are being given greater importance. So is a mother's own need to return to work. There are many choices. You may work part-time, as a temp, freelance or start your own business. You might reverse roles with your partner. You could work on short-term contracts for jobs different from those you trained for. You could try flextime, jobshares, a career break or, of course, you could work full-time.

Many of these options are due to the use of technology. Companies are starting to value employees in whom they have invested time and money.

1994 - INTERNATIONAL YEAR OF THE FAMILY

The increase in the number of working mothers is one of the greatest changes to affect families. In 1975, 47.5% of mothers with children under 18 held paying jobs. By 1994, that figure had risen to 68.4%. More than two out of three mothers were working. In 1994, 60.4% of mothers with at least one child under six was working. But more than three out of four mothers (76%) of children between 6 and 17 were working!

They do not have to be wasted or lost to another company. Evidence suggests that many working mothers now work from a home office. Companies provide them with a computer, phone and fax in their own homes. They may expect a personal visit once a week or not at all. Once the home office has been set up, companies enjoy a decrease in overhead. For the employees, a home office can ease many practical and financial pressures. You have shorter trips to pick up and drop off children. Your work hours can be flexible; your clothes, more casual. But you do lose the social contact an office can provide.

Returning to Work Full-Time

This might seem like a tiring option, but many women choose it. Workplace childcare centers are springing up in some areas to serve the growing demand of working parents. One problem with working full-time is that you may feel you aren't allowed to acknowledge you have a family. It can seem as if you have to deny this part of yourself in order to get along.

A Career Change

Sylvette thought that when she went back to work, she would change from being a computer consultant to doing something for her community. She enrolled in a counseling course. Nikki was 8 months old when she started. *"I could study with a baby, but it was hard. I chose the full-time track, to get it done in one year. I thought I could get away with not using the library when I studied. But it was hard for a while.*

"There was a lot of work during the second semester. I managed OK during the first semester, because Rob had Nikki on Saturday mornings. That gave me some time. But it was still hard to be in the same house if she was crying downstairs. In the second semester I needed more time, so it got harder.

"Before we had Nikki, we thought we'd share roles. But somehow it ended up with me doing most of the work. When I started at college things balanced out somewhat, because Rob had to do more. I wouldn't do the classes and everything else. He had to get more involved.

"The other side of that were the problems that Rob faced. I had to work on weekends. I was just too tired to work in the evenings."

Debbie has two daughters, aged 8 and 6. She works as a volunteer at her daughters' school, helping out with reading and sewing in the classrooms. She also works as a house cleaner: *"I like to earn some money to pay for the extras in our life. I like to get nice things for the girls. Also, if I didn't do this, we wouldn't have money to go out. My money is what we save for that sort of thing; my husband's is for the day-to-day running of the home.*

"My work is exhausting. I really have to have some energy left when the girls come home from school. I like to be involved with them then. But often I'm too tired to cook.

"If you work, your whole day is longer. You still have to do your own housework at the end of the day. And you also have to get their school stuff ready.

"But I don't want to go back to any other sort of work until the girls are in their teens. I'm qualified for better-paying work. But if I worked full-time I wouldn't be able to give my children the time they need. If I got a nanny or a sitter I'd have to give all my money to them."

Karen is married to Ron. They have two children, aged 5 and 2: *"Before I had the children, I had a good job in a printing company. I wouldn't have left except that I was pregnant. They did offer me the choice of going back. But I didn't know anyone who could look after my son. I wouldn't leave him with a stranger. I know I wouldn't be able to relax if he were with a sitter. My mom lives nearby but she's too old to take care of a young child.*

"I was happy to stop working. But I have to admit that when you stop, you can become brain-dead. That's what being with children all the time can do to you. After my second child, John, was born, I got a job at a bar five minutes down the road. It was simple, and I really did enjoy it. But the late nights were tough because John wasn't a great sleeper. I found that job was a great release. It was busy and we had fun. I did it for three or four nights a week. At the time, Ron was at college or at football practice

on the other nights. We didn't see very much of each other. But we both knew it wouldn't be that way for long."

Career Break

For some, like Nina, the answer is a career break: *"I was working in marketing and product development. When I was five weeks' pregnant I was offered a promotion. I thought it over, then took the job. I told my employers I was pregnant. I tried to be as helpful as I could. But the more I thought about it, the more I wanted a break. I applied for, and was offered, a 'career break.' I felt I got it because I had skills that they valued. But also because I was honest with them about my pregnancy.*

"The career break in my company could be for up to five years. Anyone could apply, not just women. And a contract would guarantee a job of the same status and salary as before —but not always the same job.

"If I hadn't been offered the break, I would have quit the job. So it's been very good for me. It gives me a fall-back option if something happens to my husband, like an accident or a layoff.

"I think it's important to be at home with my children. I'm not sure if this break will be long enough for me. I like them to feel secure and have a routine. And I don't want anyone else to bring them up. Five years is OK if you are only having one child. But if you have two or three, it's not enough if you want to wait till the youngest is at school.

"My contract says I have to go in for two weeks each year, to keep up with training and so on. I really enjoy it. On the last visit, I was asked to take on some work at home. My instinct was to say yes, but in the end I didn't do it. I just didn't want to split my attention!"

Part-time Work

This covers many options, from one day a week to 30 hours a week. If you can earn enough to meet your needs, it can be a good choice.

Some people like the status of part-time work. It can raise their self-esteem. The hours they aren't working give them time to get to know people nearby and to be with their children.

The trouble with part-time work is finding good jobs. Sometimes you can return to a previous job at the same level. But part-time work has long been the domain of the female, low-paid worker.

Many are told that their jobs can't be done part-time, that they have to be on site. But this may not always be true. Laura says: *"Mainly, you have to communicate. If you aren't there, people need to know when they can reach you. You have to let them know."*

You might dream of working in-between breastfeeding the baby and playing with her. But it isn't always as simple as that.

Penny relates: *"Every parent who has tried to work from home will come up with stories of the problems they faced. And, given the constant nature of children and the demands of working from home, they may all be true.*

"I was on the phone to a CEO who was giving me his comments on the latest draft of a contract I'd been working on. My 2-year-old son came in, shouting for me to help him with his overall buckles.

"'Go away,' I hissed. I threw maternal concern to the wind as I tried to preserve my professional image.

"'But I need to do a poo,' he wailed.

"'Then wait just a minute.' (At this point I tried to push him under the desk.)

"'But. . .'

"'Wait!'

"'But it's coming out!'

"'Is there a problem?' asked the CEO.

"'None at all,' I said. 'Afternoon talk show on the radio.'

"I have also weathered:

"—my daughter's lost pacifier falling out of a folder during a meeting. This might have been ignored, had I not fallen on it with delight, crying, 'At last, a peaceful night!';

"—expressed breast milk leaking from the bottle in my briefcase onto a computer disk, also in my briefcase. The sticky disk then blocked up my disk drive. This confused the computer repairmen. And also it smelled horrible . . . for weeks and weeks."

Rita is working part-time from home. She works 850 hours a year, and can arrange her hours as she wishes, to fit in with her two children. She just has to go into the office four days a month, which she enjoys. *"I don't feel as valued, working from home. Other people know I'm back if I go in once a week."* Because she has a yearly target of hours to meet, she can arrange her schedule so she doesn't work during school vacations. *"My main problem is I feel guilty if I take a break. It's the sort of thing you don't think twice about when you're in an office."*

Flextime

This option is becoming more popular. It worked for Alex. Although she has to work 37 hours a week, she can do it when she likes: *"This is a good compromise. I can get up one or two mornings a week and go into work at about 6:30 am. I'm home for the children by midafternoon and at bedtime, which matters to me."*

Self-employed

Some parents want to work again very badly. They may need extra income, or perhaps they want to get more out of life than caring for the children. But they are not prepared to leave the children. So they make other plans.

Lindsay wanted to work, but wanted to look after her children: *"I've always made clothes for family and friends, so it was easy to start selling them. I used a party-plan system. I invited friends or held coffees where my clothes were for sale. I would take the orders and make the clothes in the evenings.*

"When my second son was born, it got harder to stay organized. Spare time was reduced because of the baby. The orders took longer to finish. I felt bad about keeping people waiting. So I cut back again, sticking just to family and friends. Although I made less money, this is one of the things I like about this type of work. You can do it at your own pace.

"I want to be close to my children while they are young. When we decided to have children, we agreed that I would care for them during those early years.

"As Greg has gotten older, I've started selling children's books. I can take the children along with me. I do miss my colleagues and the social life of work. But I have a supervisor I can talk things through with, and that helps."

Phoebe worked in a high-pressure, stressful communications company for a number of years. Then she learned she was pregnant: *"During my pregnancy and maternity leave I worked hard to establish freelance contacts. I wanted to become a self-employed editor rather than going back to work part-time. A week before the date I was due to return I took the plunge.*

"I had arranged for childcare for my 6-month-old baby, Rose, for two days a week. This gave me two open days to work and the rest of the week to enjoy being a mother. The problems soon became clear. But I stuck to my plan. When Rose was ill, the childcare center couldn't take her. At those times I'd lose my two days. Then I had to work at other times to meet my deadlines, including weekends."

Being self-employed can give you a sense of freedom and control. But it can also be insecure and lonely. And work can intrude on your family life. But with new technology it will become a more popular work option for many women.

Role Reversal

For some parents, this seems to be the best answer to childcare problems. And it may suit their own views on working and not working.

Lana and Nick found this change was forced upon them. Nick's job was very stressful. He had a lot of traveling to do. One day he had a breakdown. He went home and has never been back. The question was what to do next. His wife Lana worked as a freelance consultant. They decided to try role reversal.

"I didn't know whether I'd have the patience," says Nick. *"But I've learned that if I can get through the day, and I don't expect to get too much done, then I'm doing OK."*

Their two children are now 2-1/2 years old and 3 months. When Lana works away from home, they all go with her, when they can. Nick is there holding the baby to pass over to her at lunchtimes for breast-feeding. *"It's working for me. I don't have to commute. I'm seeing more of the children. I have more time to spare. And my life is less stressful. I'm happy in this role. I thought there would be more time, but there isn't much left over."*

Lana is delighted that Nick cares for the children. *"I think other men who hear about him think: You lucky so-and-so. The more we thought about it, the more it seemed like a good plan. He'd always wanted to stop working early."* Other people, though, have found it harder to accept this role reversal, including their parents. But both Nick and Lana wouldn't change it. *"I am surprised how easy it is for me to look after a baby—it's given me new knowledge,"* Nick says.

And Lana: *"I could miss them when I'm away. But I relish the time without them. I paint my toenails."*

Chapter 2

Talking about Feelings

No matter what your reason for going back to work, or what kind of work you choose, this time in parents' lives arouses strong feelings. These mixed emotions affect self-esteem, relationships and future plans. The impact can be negative, positive, or both.

Other parents' stories may help. They show there are no rights and wrongs. Parenthood is unique to each parent.

Parents' Stories

Sue had a very difficult birth with her first child. And the bonding process wasn't helped by Abby's "clicky hip," which was in a cast. *"My mother came to help me when Abby was born. That was great. But soon the time came when my husband went back to work and my mother went home. I was very lonely and depressed. We were new in town, so I had no contacts. I didn't know our neighbors. I got so depressed that after a while I started drinking. One day John came home early and I was already drinking. That's how bad it had gotten. Doing nothing else besides being a mother was so awful for me that I couldn't wait to get back to work. I couldn't stand the loneliness. I'd been on my own before my marriage at the age of 30. By the age of 31 I was losing myself in motherhood in a small town.*

"So I went back to work full-time as a teacher as soon as I could. It was such a relief! The childcare people gave me confidence. They were very calm. And the school was close by. I felt it was better for Abby, too. And of course, being a teacher, I could pick her up at about 3:30 pm. I was pleased to go back, but then John's job moved him to the city. The good news was that we were nearer to John's parents. But I had other news, too. I had to give up my job. And then, before Abby's first birthday, I learned I was pregnant.

When Helen was born, it wasn't like with Abby. Because of an anal fissure I had to be very careful about pushing. I had to have an episiotomy. Other than that there were no problems. The baby was fine. We were able to get closer and the breastfeeding went well. Those first six weeks were so different. But it made me see how hard it had been for me last time. I had been in agony compared to this. I realized what I had been through with Abby.

I nursed Helen for eight months. Although things were easier, I was bored at home with a toddler and a baby. I found some work teaching part-time. Abby went to a childcare center in the mornings, and either my mother or John's mother would have the two of them in the afternoons. Later on, Helen went to a sitter. I used to cry when I left her but she never did. My mother thought what I was doing was wrong. She'd say, 'I hope you won't regret this later.' I knew I had to do it for my own sanity. I'd started teaching late and I wanted to get back to it.

"I also needed to be back at work because of my relationship with my husband. We had met, got engaged very quickly, and before we knew it, I was up to my ears in children. I was getting little sleep and I was grouchy. I had low self-esteem at the time. We didn't communicate well during those years. But I felt that I should not be a homemaker only. John was younger than me. All of a sudden he had a wife, a mortgage and kids. My mother used to say, 'You must make an effort. No husband wants to come home to a tired wife and no dinner.' But I had to feed the children, bathe them and put them to bed. To me, married life was all about bringing up children.

I think that because we were having such a rough time, I needed to hold onto my job. I went back to work full-time as soon as I could, and our marriage has lasted."

Elizabeth found that being a single parent can be tough if you want to work. *"My parents live in the Middle East, where I had lived since I was four. I went over to stay with them when Shawn was almost 2 years old, and I was offered a job in a childcare center. Over there, it's not enough to be qualified for a job. You really have to earn it by showing you can do it. I had worked with children with disabilities and had been a nanny. I also had my own little girl. So I jumped at the chance of this job.*

"Both my parents were working over there. I arranged for childcare for Shawn too, in a different room than the one I was in. She settled in well.

"It wasn't hard to decide to take the job. I wanted to do it partly to get away from Shawn for a little while. Don't get me wrong, but sometimes it's good to have a break, no matter how much you love your child.

"I didn't choose to be a single parent. But while you miss out on support from the father of your children, I think an extended family is twice as important. They are the ones that I get true support from, even though we have our ups and downs. I'm back in the United States now and I miss them a lot.

"I came back because I had met somebody. I thought we were going to get married. But by the time we got home, his family had turned him against me. So here I am, with a new baby, having to live on welfare. I'd love to be working, but I can't afford childcare for two children. There's a lot of resentment about people not working. But they don't know how hard it is to pay for childcare. So I'm going to study and try to train for something. I can't wait to start working again."

For Alex, motherhood gave her a new view of her life as a working woman: *"I think I've changed so much since having children and more so after each baby. I've learned that the company won't collapse without me. You know how you think that no one else could ever do your job? Maternity leave has shown me my presence isn't crucial.*

"I don't get so nervous, either. I'm less uptight. I think that's because I'm able to see things in a wider context. It seems to me this has made me a better manager. I'm more human, which helps because I've got 16 people reporting to me.

"I don't really separate work and home. Lots of people think of other things while they are at work. So why not think about your family? I don't see them as two separate parts of my life. I'll take work home to be with the family. Or I'll call the nanny during the day to see how the children are.

"Sales and marketing is quite a 'young' profession. There are more single, childless people than there are mothers. I'm not torn about partying with them. I really don't have too much in common with them. I'd rather go home than go to office parties.

"When I was childless, I used to stay late. When I first went back to work I felt guilty about not staying late any more. Now I really feel that quality is better than quantity.

"I think fathers may run into more problems with not staying late. If their partner has just had a baby, they're still expected to be at work until 7 pm. It's easier for a mother to say no if she's breastfeeding, or has to pick up her child from childcare."

Marcy tried to do it all but had to stop: *"I didn't decide to return to work. It just happened. We had been trying for a baby for two years. We'd been to the fertility clinic, but nothing happened. I was having weekly scans, which became depressing. My whole life was overrun by it.*

"So I tried to accept that children were once in the picture, but now they weren't. It helped to focus my mind on work and my career. Of course, as soon as I did this I became pregnant. It was hard to believe and I thought something would go wrong. I told myself that I'd have the baby, have a couple of weeks off and then go back to work.

"I was going along so fast that I never stopped to think how much time caring for this child was going to take. I guess I thought I'd rock it under the table while I worked.

"Although we'd wanted a baby for so long, now one was on the way I was determined it wouldn't change my life. When I had her, I was on a high. Nothing happened to shake my belief that it could work—you could combine motherhood with a busy career. I was back at work full-time when Rebecca was just 3 months old. It was great for a while. Then I started to notice I was getting upset by the pushing and shoving on the subway. And there were issues like starting Rebecca on solids. It all seemed happen at once and I was getting more tearful. I thought maybe I'd work part-time, but I wanted to finish the project I had started. Suddenly depression took over. I lost all my energy.

"I'm sure hormones caused a lot of the postnatal depression. But there were also lots of pressures on me. My husband thought he was going to

lose his job. I also felt very guilty about getting pregnant. I had just gone from freelancer to salaried employee. And although my boss said don't worry, we'll look after you, I felt bad about messing them up.

"The pressure on me to hold the whole thing together was enormous. I was taking on too many roles. I didn't wobble at all until the crisis passed. The pressure on Phil's job ended, and then I cracked. It just shows that you keep going until you can stop.

"I was in and out of the hospital for six months. I felt ashamed for letting everything go. Rebecca stayed with me and a local childcare center kept her place open for her until she could go there. Phil was great, but he never told his boss what was happening. They might have given him leave to look after Rebecca, but who knows.

"We were the first of our friends to have a baby and didn't know what to expect. Now my best friend is pregnant. I tell her, don't put yourself under pressure. I wish someone had told me that. I went back to work for three days a week after I got out of the hospital.

"Now I have two children and things are better. Phil is earning so much more, and our marriage has matured. I plan to go back to work. But I've learned that I can't work full-time and parent full-time."

Penny, too, was convinced that life would be the same: *"When you have your first baby, you don't know how it will change your life. You think you can do all the same things. I found life at home very hard during those first few winter months. I felt cooped up with Ben. And I hadn't built up a support network. I was happy to go back to work, I must admit.*

"Addie was born when Ben was four. By that time I had joined a working mothers' group. My ideas about children had changed, through contact with other working mothers and the pleasure of having Ben. He was more fun by now, wanting to talk to you, read to you and so on. I left my job when Addie was born. The family had become more important. I feel now that children need you more as they get older."

Lydia's return to work filled her with horror. *"Danny was born six weeks early. I was shell-shocked from having him come so soon and from the C-section. I had problems breastfeeding and felt very depressed. I work in a bank. We had a bank mortgage, so I knew I had to go back. But the thought of returning filled me with dread.*

"My attitude had changed overnight. Suddenly the job wasn't worthwhile. It had no value, it was just a job. Before, I hadn't really thought about it. But now I was convinced that bringing up a child was far more important than any other job.

"I was reluctant to go back. Fortunately the bank was flexible about my hours. It looked as though I could fit my part-time work into three days, if I worked through most of my lunch hours.

"But then, three weeks before I was due to go back, my husband Sam was laid off. It looked like I'd have to go back full-time but all my instincts said 'no.' The closer the time came, the more convinced I was I didn't want to miss out on my baby's growing up.

"We managed to work out my hours. In the end we still had enough money to live on because Sam got some money after his layoff. My mother offered to look after Danny when I was working. That meant we had no childcare costs. It helped me to know he was with her, not a stranger. I could cope with working for three days, because I knew I'd have four days with him. I was spending more time with him than away from him.

"The first time I called my mom from work, I heard him crying. I knew he was OK. I had just picked a bad time to call.

"I had to make myself not phone. I knew my mom would phone if she needed me. Being back at work isn't as bad as I expected. At first you feel like you're two people. The old team thinks you're the same person, but you're not. You're more laid back. I try not to talk about Danny, but he is the whole focus of my life. It's nice when someone does ask. But then I worry in case I talk about him too much."

Cassie's problems began when she stopped work. *"Ian was 7 months old when I went back to work. First I did three days a week as a computer consultant. But then I worked full-time for 14 months and it nearly killed me. It wasn't just the work. The company had moved 25 miles away. The distance was the problem. Then they told me I either had to stay on full-time or leave. I had no choice but to leave.*

"Although I'm glad I left, I wish I'd been able to plan it better. Ian was 2-1/2 years old when I left. He'd been in childcare. He was happy there, and he found it tough to lose his friends. I think it was hard for him to adjust to the change in his life. He was bored at home with just me and I was too. I tried to get to know people in the neighborhood, but neither of us fitted in well.

"Looking back, I should have planned something else for both of us. But I was worn out by the job, so I was glad to stop. I would say to someone else, before making any moves, think about the timing if you do decide to give up work. Think about how you will fill your day. Think about yourself and what you will do. Don't just think about your child."

Carolyn went back sooner than she would have liked. *"There is no doubt about it—I didn't want to go back to work when I did. But we were in debt. Moving to a cheaper house wouldn't have helped, because the value of ours had dropped so much since we bought it. So there was no other option.*

"I would have waited until Tom was at school as well as Mary, but that wasn't possible. I'd had plans to go back to school and become a school teacher for the primary grades. But I didn't get the chance. I work at a college, and I had heard on the grapevine there was work around. So I felt I had to take it when it was offered.

"I feel like there's someone with a whip behind me saying, faster, faster! I do teach 7 hours a week. But the preparation takes three times as long. I can only do that when the children are in bed. There is a high personal cost to all this preparation. I have no time to myself.

"I also have this constant fear in the back of my mind. What will I do if they are ill?

"The strange thing is, even though I didn't want to go back, now that I've started work again, I couldn't give it up. It's awakened me again. When we were broke and I wasn't working, I had a terrible sense of impotence. No matter how hard I tried, I couldn't make any difference. Working has helped my self-esteem. I like to be able to contribute to the house."

Chapter 3

Finding a Balance between Work and Home

Most people find becoming a family changes their lives. During your first few weeks of parenthood it is hard to think about doing anything except looking after the baby. Newborn care is time-consuming. Very often mothers feel as though they have changed in basic ways. Different things become important.

How Your Working Life May Change

So how does that feel when you go back to work? Can you focus on something else besides the baby? How do parents strike a balance between working hard and running a stable home? What are the changes you may notice in your working life? What are the problems? And what are the answers?

One change is the daily routine. You have to find childcare. More people are involved in all your plans and that changes things. You need to

---

CHANGES

You can't stop for a drink after work with your friends when it's someone's birthday, unless you make plans first.

You can't stay that extra hour to finish a project that is nearly done.

You spend your lunch hours buying diapers and pajamas rather than perfume and magazines.

You can't admit you are exhausted after being up all night because your baby had colic.

You spend your breaks dashing to the restroom with your breast pump.

You are itching to get home starting at 4:30 in the afternoon because you miss your baby so much.

Change can be positive too:

You enjoy office gossip now. It gives you a chance to separate from children.

You may feel more motivated than before. More depends on keeping your job.

You enjoy the company of your colleagues. You know that parenting can be lonely.

keep these people informed about your plans. That makes it harder to do things at the last minute. This fact can be hard to adjust to. Other scheduling issues to think about: Your childcare people need to know when you are going on vacation. Your child has to be picked up by a certain time. You can't leave the house in just 15 minutes anymore if you oversleep.

Problems in Finding a Balance

Leaving Your Baby

How long does it take to believe that your baby is OK without you? For some parents, coming home after the first day and finding a happy baby is enough. They can start to relax and enjoy being away from the baby. Other parents take longer than that. Some suffer from separation anxiety. It may take time to stop worrying. Alicia says, *"I went back to work three weeks before I had to. I knew it would be a busy time, and I wouldn't have a chance to think about Fernando as much. I think it worked. I also traded those three weeks for three weeks in the future for a trip we have planned when he is a year old."*

Kelly made sure to adjust slowly. She arranged to go in for mornings only for two weeks, to get both of them used to the changes. *"But when I went back I felt awful and it didn't stop.*

"Sometimes it was not so bad and sometimes it was awful. I was racked with guilt. If Stephanie was ill, I blamed myself for working full-time."

Kari admits: *"Leaving was awful. I couldn't take Jo to the sitter for the first couple of days, even though I liked her. The first morning at work, the personnel manager knew I was on the edge, and didn't push me. After that I was fine, and Jo was fine too. My sitter would call me at work if Jo had been upset and let me know that she'd settled down."*

Saying Goodbye

This depends on the age of your baby. When they are very little they may be asleep when you go. Some parents prefer a quiet exit, because it often means the baby or child doesn't get upset. But, as children get older, they may cling to you more. They don't know when you will be going, and they may not let you out of their sight.

When you say goodbye to them, you make your leaving clear. It may upset them and you too. But then the child knows what is going on. She will get a good-bye kiss and a hug from you. She'll get used to that routine. She'll also learn that you are going anyway, whether she cries or not. And that you always come back. Then you may find leaving easier.

To Phone or Not to Phone?

Some parents can't stop thinking about babies and start thinking about work if the last thing they saw was their baby crying in someone else's arms. Chances are that the baby stopped crying the minute you left. But you don't know that. You may have spent the next hour worrying about your baby's welfare.

If you phone, you may pick a moment when your baby is crying for some other reason. It won't seem that way to you. You could ask your caregiver to give you a call when the baby stops crying, until you start to relax about it.

If your baby is at a childcare center, you might want to phone there. If a baby is crying at the other end, the chances are it's not yours. Often one of the staff can look in on your baby and put your mind at rest.

What about Guilt?

When I was talking to mothers about this book, an equal number *didn't* feel guilty about working as did. There is a strong sense from some parents that they enhance their own lives, and those of their children, by working. They would be stifled by being at home all the time. They need the outlet of work. They feel it helps them be better mothers.

Of course, these mothers may miss their children. Or they may feel they are missing out on some of the fun of being a parent. But they don't feel guilty about it.

Alex did feel guilty about leaving her little girl. Some of the comments she got at work made her feel worse. *"The first time I went back, people really hurt me. They said I was just doing it for the money and what about my kids. Some people have strong feelings. They think they have to say something. It worried me. At the time I was a little confused myself and didn't know if I was harming her. But Melissa turned out fine. I get along well with her. I know that I'm doing the right thing."*

Ann went back to work when her baby was 2-1/2 weeks old. Her parents were looking after him. She burst into tears at her first job because she felt so guilty. Then her husband Michael pointed out that she had left him in the next-best possible hands. *"I felt it was better to leave him with family, but it upset me at the time. I had to break myself in gently when I left him with a sitter for the first time. But he was fine."*

Work, Babies and Fatigue

Babies may not sleep through the night for months, or even years, for some. There will be times when fatigue will seem to consume you.

Sandy spent a lot of her early weeks back at work exhausted. *"Alexa had trouble with her ear when I went back to work at a new job. That meant she could be awake every two hours during some nights. I was just a zombie. But nobody seemed to notice."*

Susie's son wasn't a good sleeper: *"I used to be a wreck. But you manage somehow because you're at work. I'm convinced it's why I never lost weight. I used to eat to keep myself awake. I thought if I ate something, I'd feel better."*

Kari adds: *"Now I am always tired. I never have enough sleep. We take turns sleeping in on the weekend. I didn't used to feel like this all the time. But it's what you get for working and commuting too. When I get home, I don't stop. Jo doesn't go to bed till 8:30 pm, so you can't cook till then. We don't eat until about 9:15 pm. By the time you've cleared the dishes, the evening's gone. But instead of going to bed then I want a little time to relax. I always go to bed later than I should."*

"Just" a Part-Timer

In some jobs, you have to be seen to work long hours to move ahead. In some companies nobody leaves work at five, even if their work is done. Leaving on the dot is not the thing to do.

So where does that leave working parents who have to get away on time for their children? For parents who go back to work part-time, the long-hours culture simply isn't worth it. But that doesn't make it easy to choose part-time work.

Heather had trained as an accountant eight years before her daughter Olivia was born. *"It had taken me years to get where I was. I didn't want to give up. I also wanted some life of my own. We live on a military base. I wanted some contacts away from that. I made it clear to my employer that I would be coming back. I had planned to go back full-time.*

"I went back full-time after six months. But our company wasn't doing well, and there wasn't much work. I had given up clients when I left and it was hard to build up more.

I suggested going part-time for a while, and they agreed. So I started working mornings only. It went fine for a few months. But then a big contract came up, which they wanted me to take. So I went back full-time. But I wasn't happy doing it. I had become used to working part-time. As Olivia got older, she became calmer. She wasn't such hard work, and I enjoyed her more.

"Then they offered me a partnership. They said, 'Come back to full-time work. We'll give you the training you need and in two years' time. . . .' I was tempted. I wanted to feel I had achieved something, reached the top. So I said I'd go back. But I wasn't prepared for my feelings. I reached the end of the first week having worked from 7 am until 7 pm. I knew this was how it would always be if I was going to make it as a partner. I was very tired and very grumpy. And there were so many things to be done at home. But the worst thing was that I had lost touch with Olivia already. So, I risked losing my job and said the partnership didn't interest me, if this is what it takes. It was a tough choice to make. And it was the turning point of my career. But now I had Olivia I was able to look at the other partners. Their work ruled their lives. I knew that I didn't want to live like that. They're very wealthy. But their work is everything. I have more than that now.

"They made it plain I wouldn't move up any further. But they were happy to keep me on a part-time basis for the time being, at least. They said that in a couple of years they might have to review my position.

"But then I was headhunted by a former client. I insisted on it being part-time and they agreed. They were very positive about it. They also made it clear that it could be a job for life. This was a tax job. I needed to go to their headquarters overseas to learn about their tax system. So the whole family is going on an all-expense paid trip for five months: me, my husband, Olivia and her nanny!"

Not every parent enjoyed working part-time. Laura first went back for 2-1/2 days a week: *"Work didn't interest me as much when I was back part-time. It happened slowly. I didn't notice at first. But after 6 months I felt I was treated less as a working person. I was told that I would make a* good team leader. 'But of course it's out of the question because you're working part-time.' I think it did affect my career prospects. The attitude of my colleagues didn't change, though. And my rank in the company didn't suffer."

Does working part-time make life harder for a man?

Chris works as a computer programmer. When his daughter, Hannah, was about 4 months old, he started working a 4-day week so he could spend time with her. *"I must say in my current work there's no stigma attached to working part-time. More women than men work reduced hours. But in my department of about 35, I know of two other men who have decreased their work hours. I don't have to justify working shorter hours. I'm just not expected to produce the same output as a full-time employee.*

"In this company, working part-time does not prevent promotion. You just have to be able to meet the demands of a higher post. In practice, I don't think there are many part-timers in the higher echelons of management. My own ambitions are not huge. I'm not looking for a promotion. Work is more a means to an end, for now. And I've welcomed the chance to get involved with the care of my own daughter. A number of people respect my decision to do this. I'm lucky, of course, that my partner, Sally, earns a fairly high salary and wants to share childcare."

Sometimes, people don't feel they are in the swing of things as a part-timer. Patty felt this. *"I was just coming in, doing some work and going home again. I didn't feel part of what was going on. I don't know whether the feeling came from me or the company."*

The sense of having to prove yourself as a part-timer is very common. Tanya felt it strongly. *"I took my baby in to work once or twice. She was asleep under the desk for ages. Another woman was having work done at her house. She spent lots of time talking about it on the phone. I must have done twice as much as she did. But she said that I shouldn't have bothered coming in with the baby.*

"I felt I needed to justify my presence. I kept trying to increase my workload. I was late a few times and got comments. That's why I've given up now. I'd rather work freelance and make up the time in the evenings. I don't want people to have the right to judge me about how much work I do, and when I do it."

There is also the feeling, even though you work part-time, that you have to do as much, or more, than the full-timers do. You can never be seen relaxing. Laura says: *"I felt I was putting five days into four. I didn't drink coffee in the morning. I felt like I had to justify working the shorter week."*

Amy is a doctor, and the only partner in her practice who works part-time. *"I feel like I'm not pulling my weight, even though I work 30 hours a week. But having said that, I think that my job is quite family-friendly, if stressful. In this practice, all the partners except me take on extra work, like the Well Woman clinic. But I simply don't have time to do that.*

"It means that I do feel I'm somewhat a second-class citizen. But my family comes first, and that's that."

Many parents feel they want to be back at work, but they don't want to be there all the time. As we have seen, many women feel that their careers suffer because of it. Fortunately, the situation is changing, though slowly. Job-sharing, shortened hours and working from home are becoming more accepted.

What Happens When the Children Are Sick?

"The real problem is if the children get ill." —Carolyn

"The tough thing is not having family nearby. I don't know what I'd do if she got sick." —Tanya

This is the classic problem of being a working parent. Most of the time, things run smoothly. But when a child is sick, it becomes a major problem. Some companies offer a set number of days' leave each year to allow parents time off when their children are ill. Often parents have to make their own plans.

Sue started a new job when she returned to work from having her baby. Her little girl had problems with her ear. She needed to have an ear-tube fitted. Sue didn't know if she would get the call from the hospital on her starting day. *"I had to tell work that it could happen on the first day. But they were OK about it. I made it clear at the interview that my family comes first. They know that anyway. And they were glad I'd been honest with them."*

Kari always kept a week's leave available. That way if Jo ever needed her, she would have a few days ready for that purpose. She still feels guilty sometimes, even when she feels ill herself: *"Recently when I was sick, and so was she, we stayed in bed all day. The next day she still wasn't right. I could have gone in, but I stayed at home to look after Jo. I still wasn't totally well, but I felt guilty about staying home anyway."*

Many working parents fear that if they take too much time off because their baby is sick, they might be fired. These fears may be unfounded, but rumors of it happening to others tend to haunt working parents.

If it's the sitter who is ill, you have a number of options. You might use another caregiver, a relative or a childcare center.

A support network of other local mothers can help, as Jan found. *"I have two close friends who work part-time as well. We help each other out when caregivers are ill. We even have each other's children if they are a bit under the weather. They play together so much that if one of them catches something, the others are likely to have picked it up too."*

Of course if your child is really ill it is *you* they need. *"When Katy was 10 months old she had herpes simplex. Her mouth and throat were covered with sores. She couldn't eat or drink. All she wanted was to suck at the breast and be carried around. There was no way I could work."*

Solutions

Coping with Separation

There are many ways you can make the separation easier for you and your child. But the important message is not to feel you are being childish or neurotic. Try:

COPING STRATEGIES

Checklist

1. Be happy with your childcare plans.

2. Prepare things in advance. This way the morning isn't a mad rush. Pack changing bag, change of clothes, food or anything else ahead of time.

3. Try to arrange a shorter day at first.

4. Make sure you know what you need to take—or leave behind.

5. Give your caregiver your phone number at work, and your extension number.

6. Talk to your caregiver the day before you start, when your baby isn't around.

7. Warn your employer that you may be a little late that first day.

8. Don't plan meetings for first thing in the morning.

9. Bring plenty of tissues, and your make-up, if you use it.

10. When you say you are going, take deep breath and go.

11. Find a quiet spot to have a good cry if you need to. Blow your nose and tell yourself that your child will be fine.

12. Talk over how you feel with your partner or a friend.

- Building up the time spent with the caregiver slowly.
- Start by staying with the caregiver for a while. Then, as your child gets to know the caregiver, try leaving them alone for longer periods of time.
- Leaving familiar objects with her.
- If she is going somewhere else, take along her favorite toy or blanket. Such things will make her feel more secure.
- Set up routines.

Babies and children all like routines. Routines help children know what's going on. They help children control their lives and help them feel secure. Make it a habit to explain what will happen next. Your child will understand you sooner than you think. Talking will help him or her feel more relaxed. When you get ready to go back to work, try to keep as many other things the same as you can. Don't make your child deal with any other changes at that time. And make sure that you are really happy with your childcare.

It may sound obvious. But it really does make a difference if you feel totally happy that your baby is in the right place. And she is likely to sense your feelings about the caregiver.

Negotiate

If you are not happy with the plan for your return to work, you may be able to negotiate something better.

Laura says: *"It costs an employer thousands of dollars to train someone for my kind of job (inflation management). For the company, it has to be worth retaining trained, knowledgeable people. But if you are the employee, it takes guts to ask for changes. If you're going to ask, make sure you're asking the right person. There is no point in asking someone who has no time for working mothers. My boss is a woman. She has a little girl. But she is not very supportive. She says things like, 'I never think about Rebecca.' Because she is a working mother, you would expect her to be more helpful to others and their feelings."*

On the other hand, many mothers have had more success than they expected by being firm, like Jeri: *"I'm a social worker. I was due back to work when my baby was 6 months old. But I didn't feel I would be ready by then. I was very unhappy about leaving the baby. But since this was later than the first date I was supposed to be due back, I felt I couldn't ask for any more time off.*

CHECKLIST

Checklist for Negotiating

1. Are you used to doing it? Do you feel confident about it? If not, talk to someone who is used to workplace negotiations.

2. Sit down and write out what you want.

3. Check the essential items. This gives you a few options you can lose in a compromise.

4. Try to look at it from their point of view, too. What are they likely to accept and reject?

5. Check your employment contract. Be familiar with it. They will be!

6. Be clear about what you want, but give them some choices.

7. Don't do anything rash. Be polite and well-mannered. Give yourself time to think over what has been said.

8. Think creatively. Look for as many options as you can.

9. Ask yourself what you will do if you can't get what you want.

10. You may need to prove yourself again. If they won't accept compromise now, ask if you can open the discussion again in 3 months' time.

*But I thought it through one more time and asked for another two months'
leave. We ended up compromising. My baby will be 8-1/2 months old
when I go back, which is fine by me."*

Alex believes you have to negotiate for what you want, as she did after
the birth of her second child: *"I went back two months early from my
maternity leave. I was given 10 weeks to prove I could do my job part-
time. They told me it was 'out of the question' for a manager to be part-
time. We ended up agreeing on total flextime. As long as I do my 37.5
hours a week, I can do them whenever I want. I go in very early, at 6:30
or 7 am, one or two mornings a week. This way I can leave early to be
with the children. And I can go back to work in the evenings, after they're
in bed.*

*"It's tough, but it's worth it for the children. I don't think you're ever com-
pletely happy. What I've learned is that you have to be creative and think
around the problem. And you have to be prepared to compromise."*

Being Assertive

Being assertive is all about making your objectives and your feelings
clear, in a pleasant but firm way. It's not about banging your fist on the
table, or bursting into tears when something doesn't go your way. Such
behavior only invites negative comment.

It is still hard to be accepted as an assertive, strong woman. Even today,
assertive men are seen as "powerful" and "dynamic." But assertive
women can be seen as "bossy, nagging or difficult." Don't worry about
such attitudes.

If you are not used to being assertive, it can be hard. It's even harder if
you have been away from work for a few months. It's amazing how
quickly one can lose confidence in oneself. It helps to practice being
assertive in your daily dealings. For example, if you're in a restaurant and
you are breastfeeding your baby, what would you do if someone
complained?

You need to be assertive when you negotiate your terms for going back to work. Sometimes you need to be assertive when you get back into the office, too. Frances says, *"When I went back to work, someone had taken over my desk. I was offered a place in the corner. I needed to be assertive during those first few days."*

If you have been away from the office for a few months, it is easy to feel less valued by behavior like this. You may have lost some of your confidence when you were away. And you may feel a bit rusty in the job. So you may feel they have a point. But within a few days, you are likely to be back in the swing of the office. Your colleagues will probably be glad to have you back. They'll see that you're the same person, but with an added dimension.

If you would like to learn more about being assertive, you'll find many classes that can teach you about it. Your local library may be able to refer you to them.

Being assertive is:
- Knowing what you want
- Being clear
- Listening carefully
- Being polite
- Stating your case
- Not being put off in your objective

Being assertive is not:
- Shouting
- Being rude
- Ignoring other people's views

Sharing Childcare Duties

If both you and your partner work, you may want to share the tasks of arranging for care, dropping off and picking up.

Sometimes, as Kari relates, *"More often than not John is the one who's picked her up or taken time off. It comes down to whose meetings are more important. I'm more strong-willed and say this is very important. And he often caves in.*

"One job is not more important than the other. We are both managers and we both have responsibilities. You can't just drop things willy-nilly. I can't get home by 6:30 pm when the childcare center closes, so it has to be him."

Sometimes partners go further, and work fewer hours to share the parenting, like Chris: *"I can only speak for myself. But there is no doubt that looking after Hannah for a full day each week has been great for both of us. I'm sure we get along much better because of it. I understand a lot more of what Sally has to cope with every day. Dads who don't have the time to spend with their young children miss out on a lot. I wonder if the relationship with the female partner is strengthened by being more involved, too?"*

Mary Beth and her husband are business partners, so it's easier for them to be flexible. She works two days a week: *"We try to make it either/or. It's nice after breastfeeding, when it's just the mother's task. But if one of the children were sick, it would likely be me who came home. I'm less squeamish!"*

But others agree to let the mother take charge of all things involving childcare, like Laura: *"My husband's career comes first. My job doesn't even cover the mortgage. We have an understanding, because the house wouldn't run without his job. He sees things from a financial point of view. I think he's the loser. But the long-hours culture means it's hard for him to keep the respect of his colleagues if he doesn't put in the time they do."*

Although it has become more common for men to provide childcare, they are still more likely to receive attention for their efforts than women. Stu, a bartender, thrives on the attention he gets from his children's friends. *"They think it's great I'm at home during the day and part of the neighborhood childcare circle."*

It isn't easy to balance the tasks. It depends on a number of factors, like:

- Your feelings about going back to work
- Your partner's feelings about your return to work
- Attitudes and support at both places of work
- Other sources of support

If you are a single parent, you will probably shoulder all the duties yourself. It helps to have a supportive family. Being a single parent means you may need your workplace and the company of your colleagues to balance caring for your child alone.

Most parents agree that having children changes their lives. But after the first few years, old habits do return. You *can* find a balance between your working life and family life.

Chapter 4

Time Off—
Life as a Family

Working and running a home leaves little time off for either partner. There are often household chores to be done: cleaning, washing, shopping and more. So far, the focus of this book has been on work. But becoming a family is also about having time off together.

Add to that the fact that you may not have seen much of your children during your working hours. You will want to spend time with them. And you need time with your partner. That often gets put to one side when babies arrive. How can you do all of this, and relax too?

Shared Parenting

When both partners work, household chores should be divided equally. But, in practice, the woman takes care of childcare in most cases. Her partner may support her by helping out with picking up the children or other tasks.

Kari recalls: *"Last summer, John was very busy at work and played in a baseball league. I said I wanted a day when he does everything and I get pampered. He's never, ever, done the whole day. He's done work days, but never a whole day on the weekend. I want him to see the ups and downs.*

"At the working mothers' group I attend, I was talking about our setup. I said I drop Jo off and John picks her up. And I said that he's promised me that he will pick her up on time. Someone said to me, 'What do you mean, he's promised you? That means it's your job and you have to make sure he does it.' It's true. He makes the commitment to me. But in the end I'm the one who is responsible. I think most working mothers would admit they are the ones who feel responsible. I do."

Sometimes you can start off with shared tasks, then drift. Cathy said, *"My husband doesn't help around the house. But he does like to cook, so he often makes dinner. I think the thought of shared parenting has faded over time. He was all for it at first, but less so now. But he does come home at lunchtime. So he gets to see the children then."*

Sometimes breastfeeding can interfere with the sharing of tasks. Some fathers might not bother to get up during the night if they feel they aren't needed. But other fathers give bottles of expressed milk at night to help the mother get more rest. Or the father may get up and bring the baby to the mother for nursing.

Shared Parenting—A Learned Skill

Most of us grew up with certain assumptions. We may select certain roles without much thought. A lot of our role models come from our parents. They lived in a different time. So when we think about shared childcare, we need to think about our assumptions and those of our partner. It's a good place to start.

It helps to talk things over where assumptions may have been made. Male partners and their duties have changed a great deal in the last 30 years, though some people may not think this is true. Also, what looks like sharing to one couple won't seem fair to another. Today fathers may cook meals on a regular basis, or bathe the children. Thirty years ago this was unheard of. But not all people change at the same pace. Just be sure you don't make assumptions about your own relationship. It helps to sit down and talk about what is important to you both.

Looking at a Situation Differently

"It makes me mad that women are criticized for being scatterbrained or bad drivers. It's because we do so many different things at the same time. And we do most of them well. No wonder things get forgotten. But men are allowed to ignore things, like when you're lying in bed, and the baby is crying. He will turn over and not respond. The woman always cracks first," says Natalie.

This type of friction can develop because each partner believes the other isn't pulling his or her weight, or they believe too much is expected of them. There was no need to talk about this until, all of a sudden, there is a new baby. Then the couple's role-model roots suddenly appear, along with certain assumptions. Sometimes people aren't really aware of their own assumptions until they become parents. Once you perceive yourself as a mother or a father, you may suddenly step into your parents' shoes. You may behave like your parents without having come to a reasoned conclusion that it's the best way. Have you ever heard children imitate their parents, wagging fingers, or copying those timeless expressions? That's what can happen when you become a parent. You find yourself repeating all those silly things that your parents said to you—*that's my girl . . . wait and see . . . .*

It's easy to have an equal relationship when you both earn a salary, work full-time and have no children. How will you feel if, because you stay at home with your baby, for a few weeks or a few years, you are cast in the role of the homemaker?

Who Does What?

If you want to share parenting, think about what needs to be done. Allocate tasks according to the times you are around, or what you are best at doing, or what you prefer to do. Nobody wants to do the jobs they hate. But you can list what needs to be done and decide what you can do.

You could list these tasks in order of preference, with number one being most favored. Those jobs that only you like, you do. And those jobs that only your partner likes, the partner does. And those jobs you both hate, you could trade off on a weekly basis.

Many couples find that having someone to help in the house eases the pressures. Even though money is tight, Karen pays a neighbor to do the ironing: *"Just looking at the laundry basket used to make me feel irritable. Now I drop it off on the way to work and pick it up later. It's worth $8.00 an hour not to have to start ironing at 10:00 at night."*

Janet accepts that she is in charge of childcare, which suits her and her husband very well. But she expects him to take on other roles. *"I arrange for the childcare. I pay the nanny and outline the childcare duties. But I do the washing, and he does the shopping."*

Sue is happy that she and her partner share tasks, but she says, *"There is nothing he can't do instead of me. It puts too much of a burden on me otherwise. One of the best things I ever did was explain to him that he doesn't* help *with the chores, we* share *them."*

Unexpected Events

Sometimes an event places people in roles they hadn't wanted at all. Joan discovered this when her husband was laid off. *"Ted helped out more at*

home. He learned he was doing it for our joint needs, not just to help me out. He is working again now, but shorter hours. He can work a lot more from home, take the children to school and so on. I see his relationship with them warming and improving all the time. It really feels more like a family.

"It was hard to give up running the home at first. I had been in charge. I had to accept we were sharing this now. That meant accepting that Ted might not do things my way. He is very good, and things get done, but not as I would do them.

"Still, I am the primary wage earner, the primary child caregiver and the main cleaner. Sometimes I wish he would just quit working. He could look after the children, and I could focus more on my job. I'd be happy with that. But I know he won't."

Changing Priorities

It can put a lot of pressure on a relationship when both partners have careers. Things can become more stressful when there are young children around. For some, it makes sense to alternate the dominant career. One partner takes a back seat while caring for young children. This way you don't have to feel that you have to give up work forever.

Sue says: *"We've sort of decided his job comes first. So if Alexa were ill, I would take care of her. We never discussed it. But we both feel happy with it. I wouldn't want to give up work completely. But I'm not going to focus on my career until the children are in school."*

Some couples plan such career changes to suit a family. Jenny worked long hours in the very demanding field of medicine. Her husband's job involved lots of travel: *"Two stressful careers in one family would have been too much. Once the children were born I moved into part-time work. My career is on hold for a while."*

Not every job is so flexible. But, as more women attempt to combine family and career, it's to be hoped more employers will create "family-friendly" alternatives for employees.

Partnership Pressures

No doubt, having a family puts pressure on a relationship, even when it enhances it in a broader sense. There is less time to go around. The time that used to be spent relaxing with one other person is often spent chasing children to bed, reading endless bedtime stories or getting ready for the next morning. This doesn't leave much time for the couple to maintain their closeness. On the other hand, if you are both working, you may want to spend as much time as you can with the whole family. So where do you find the time? How do you make time for it all? How do you prevent the symptoms of stress—tiredness, lack of libido, loss of intimacy, and conflicts over children?

Sharing the same goals can help reduce such pressures.

Laura: *"It was a mutual decision for me to return to work. He really felt it was right for me. The only thing he wanted to change was the method of childcare. We got a nanny, so there's not so much housework to do."*

Heather: *"My husband was very supportive about me going back to work. He wants me to have contacts outside the house. He's always respected me for that. And he wants it to stay that way. He doesn't want to lose the person that he married."*

Amy: *"My partner encouraged me to go back to work. He didn't like the thought of me being concerned only with household issues. I felt the same way, but less so now with four children. When the first two were little, I felt frustrated with no one to talk to during the day. But I feel that four keep me very busy. And they are more fun all the time. I am more involved in reading-and-learning skills. With four, there are more built-in social outlets, more structure to the day."*

Time with Your Partner

When both of you are working, there is, as Tanya points out, a pecking order of who deserves to sleep in on the weekend. It's easy to start counting. *"It all comes down to how hard have you worked. 'I've worked harder than you.' 'How hard did you work the week before?' It's as if there are bargaining chips. 'I've got to go to work in the morning, so you've got to get up too . . . ' and on and on."* Prevent arguments. Work out a flexible schedule.

Lindsay says it isn't easy to find time to be with her husband. *"John and I don't have much time together. Often by the time the work is done, all we can do is stare at the TV for an hour before we go to bed. That's why we try to keep our weekends for the family. Before Christmas it was hard. I had to go to a lot of craft fairs with my books, so Sundays became very precious. But this is the way I want to do it. And I know that whatever I want to do, John will support me."*

TIME

Time with Your Partner

- Hire a babysitter once every week or two. You may be tired but it's worth having some time alone with each other.

- Go to bed early—together.

- Plan to spend time together, away from the TV, on a regular basis.

- Talk through issues when they come up, but not when you could lose your temper.

- Listen to what your partner says. You may not be the only one who is tired or has been working hard.

- Sit somewhere where no children's toys are visible. Or better still, keep one room free of train sets, doll houses and so forth.

Single Parenting and Support

If you are one of a couple, you can share the household chores. If you are a single parent, then the burden is all on you. Add to that the financial pressure of only one salary coming in, and life can become very stressful.

Working may only bring in a little more money than you may receive on welfare. And childcare costs can be large. So why should a single mother work? Why go out to work if you don't get any more money than you would staying at home with the children? In the first place, there are limits on how long you can collect welfare payments. Also, a job can be a lifeline to a mother who is the sole caregiver for her children the rest of the time. You need to socialize, work with adults and have a break from family life, much as you love your children. Work can help you make new friends, too. There are also support groups for single parents, such as the National Organization of Single Mothers (see Resources). Many churches and temples also organize support groups for single parents.

Jean struggled to work and bring up two children under five on her own, after her husband left her: *"There were evenings after I'd put the children to bed that I just collapsed into bed myself. I felt so lonely and exhausted. I needed someone to talk to, unwind and crack a joke with. A woman at work told me about a support group for single parents. After a few more weeks of loneliness, I called them. It was great to talk to people like me."*

Getting the most out of your time as a single parent can be a challenge. Try the following:
- Ask people to make your house the place for meetings and talks.
- Find out if you have any neighbors who might babysit in return for other favors, such as shopping for them, or driving their children to school.
- Double up with other friends with children so your social life isn't wall-to-wall parenting.

Family Time

There is also the family as a whole to think about, whether you're a single parent or a couple. If the children aren't seeing a great deal of you during the week, you may want to spend time with them on the weekend. But you're tired, too. What can you do?

Good time management can ease the day-to-day pressures and allow you time to be yourself again. Try some of the following:

- Splurge on a dishwasher or freezer.
- Eat your main meal at lunchtime. Then you only need to fix a snack in the evening.
- Invest in a cleaning or ironing helper.
- Create a weekly menu before you go shopping.
- Don't shop on weekends. Have one partner do it one weekday evening with a shopping list.

- Don't take the children shopping. They get bored before you do. You may end up having to leave—only to come back again a few days later.
- Buy as much as you can through catalogs.
- If you have a nanny, get her to do as many jobs as she can. She can mail letters, pick up dry cleaning, and do all the things that can involve taking the children for a walk.
- Get a diaper service.
- Make lists and cross things off when you've done them.
- Turn off the television when you've finished watching a specific program.

Often, spending time with your children can get you charged up. It often involves exercise, which stimulates your system and gives you extra energy. The children also enjoy themselves—and we all know that happy children make for happy parents.

If you have friends with young children, try to meet with them often. The children will have playmates, and you will have other grown-ups to talk to. Such friends can be like an extended family.

Spend some time together as a couple while your friends watch all the children, then swap roles. Very often, double the number of children does *not* mean "double trouble." More kids can be *less* work.

Not many parents can say they have enough time to do all the things they want to do. Often it is one's sleep and "me" time that get left out.

Work can give you moments of time to yourself. You may travel to a meeting, spend a little longer at coffee breaks, take lunch hours when you have them. At such times your thoughts won't be disturbed by distant wailing.

Joy talks about her working days: *"I've worked both at home and in an office. I know the value of a lunch hour where you can sit and do a crossword and unwind. You don't get that when you're at home with children."*

Then there is the question of guilt. Should you feel that you want time on your own? If you are working, shouldn't you spend all your spare time with the family? *"I would like to take a couple of days off to make some curtains. But then I think that if I do have a day off, I should spend it with Jo,"* says Kari.

That's a key issue for working parents: how to find the time to do things well and meet all your needs. Still, work can be a vital part of family life. The fulfillment it brings can complete the picture for many parents. Beth sums it up: *"I know I'm a better person for working. I never had a picture of myself as a full-time mother. I give more to my children by having my work role complement my role within the family."*

Chapter 5

Thinking about Childcare

First Thoughts

Before having children, most people do not think about childcare. Why should they? After you have children, if you plan to work, the next step is to find out about childcare. You may start to think about this when you are pregnant. Or you may look at it when your youngest child has started school and you feel ready to go back to work.

Have other people in your workplace taken maternity leave and said they were coming back? Did they come back? Or did they eventually decide they preferred to spend more time at home? What were your feelings about that? Were you surprised that someone would give up a good job just to stay at home? Or were you thinking you might feel the same way?

What about parents who return to work and have to leave at a certain time to pick up their children? Sometimes it can cause resentment among the rest of the workers. But most parents agree they work harder than they did before because of the stricter hours they must keep.

When these things happen at work before you have a family yourself they don't seem to matter much to you. People sometimes try to think how they might feel when they are pregnant and make plans for the future. You might plan, for instance, when you'll come back to work, or what sort of work you might choose. But your feelings often change after the baby is born. This means that, much as you aim to be prepared for the future with the baby, sometimes emotions can put your plans "on hold." You may also think, "I know I won't feel the same once the baby is born. And because I don't know how I'll feel, I won't bother to make plans until I've had the baby and know what I want."

59

But life isn't so simple. Some plans simply can't wait until your baby is born. Many childcare centers enroll a year or so in advance. If this is what you think you might want, it may be too late to sign up by the time the baby is born. When you prepare for conflicting emotions, you have a better chance of dealing with them when the time comes.

Childcare Choices

These depend on a number of factors, including where you live, where you work and your own needs.

Local Conditions and Childcare

Childcare options may depend on where you live. When you start thinking about childcare, you need to find out what your choices are. In a rural area with no public transportation, it might be harder to hire an au pair, for example. An au pair (a young foreign student who looks after your children in exchange for living in your home) would want access to English classes and an active social life with other young people.

What about childcare centers? If you live in a city, you may find that childcare centers have long waiting lists. It's worth finding out just what your choices are.

Each of the following will be described in more detail in later chapters.

Family Day-Care Homes

A family day-care home is a home in which care is provided to a number of children. Family day-care homes are licensed in many, but not all, states. Even in states that license such homes, many are not licensed. But, licensed or not, 6-million children are cared for in such homes throughout the United States. In Canada, more than 570,000 children are cared for in regulated and unregulated family day care.

Quality childcare is measured by:
• Ratio of staff to children
• Number of children in the group
The National Association for the Education of Young Children recommends that one adult should care for no more than 4 babies. The group should not include more than 6 to 8 babies, even if there is more than one adult caregiver.

Safety First!

All states have set health-and-safety standards for childcare centers. But not all regulate family day-care homes. Standards vary by province in Canada also. Licensed care is likely safer. Make sure the childcare center or family day-care home you choose is licensed.

The 10 Best States for Childcare

In 1995 Working Mother magazine convened a national panel of 100 childcare experts in the United States for the first time. They rated each state in terms of quality, safety and commitment to childcare. They also rated them according to how many licensed childcare slots each state had in relation to the need for childcare in the state. In 1997, the 10 best states were:

California	Connecticut	Maryland	Minnesota	Washington
Colorado	Hawaii	Massachusetts	Vermont	Wisconsin

The worst childcare states were Idaho, Louisiana and Mississippi. They each permit one caregiver to care for up to 12 toddlers. These states also spend very little on childcare.

Childcare standards in Canada vary greatly by province, so a comparison is difficult to make. Call the Canada Childcare Federation for information regarding your province's standards at (613) 729-5289.

The 10 Best Cities for Working Mothers

When it comes to cities, where you live makes a big difference. Cities differ a great deal. Family-friendly cities can make your life as a working mother a lot better. In 1996, Redbook magazine rated cities in the United States according to: percent of mothers in the labor force; price of a home; quality of schools; healthful environment; and family-friendly employers.

The 10 best cities for working mothers were:

Sioux Falls, SD	Fargo, ND	Tallahassee, FL	Seattle, WA
Boulder, CC	Rochester, MN	Omaha, NB	
Madison, WI	Des Moines, IA	Raleigh-Durham, NC	

No large cities made the list.

Source: Redbook, June 1996, v187, n2, page 94(7)

In Canada, Chatelaine magazine has asked working women which cities they rated as best. The top-10 cities were:

Ottawa-Hull, Ontario	London, Ontario	Oshawa, Ontario
Sherbrooke, Quebec	Winnipeg, Manitoba	Quebec, Quebec
Saskatoon, Saskatchewan	Kitchener, Ontario	
St. John's, Newfoundland	Vancouver, British Columbia	

Source: Chatelaine, April 1994, page 51

Nanny

A nanny is likely to be young and qualified in childcare. She may have a lot of experience. Nannies may live-in or come in daily. A nanny can cost $200.00 to $400.00 or more per week, including room and board. You must also pay employment taxes. Some nannies expect a car and other benefits.

Even where jobs are scarce, many citizens of the United States and Canada prefer not to work as a nanny. But women from less-developed countries, which place greater value on domestic work, are often eager to do so.

Canada provides a 3-year visa to homecare workers from other countries. After three years of homecare work in Canada, the worker may become a Canadian citizen if she chooses.

There have been efforts in support of special visas for foreign homecare workers in the United States. But they have not been successful. Many undocumented immigrants perform low-cost domestic duties in American homes. Even though some are well-qualified, this is illegal and could lead to problems. Others are not. It may not be easy to find a qualified, legal nanny. The Child Care Action Campaign publishes a guide, *Finding and Hiring a Qualified In-Home Caregiver* (see Resources). Or contact the nonprofit American Council of Nanny Schools (see Resources).

Au Pair

"Au pair" means "on a par with." This means that an au pair should be treated like a member of the family. An au pair is most likely a young woman from Western Europe, between 18 and 25 years of age. She will live in the home for a year, perform childcare and do light housework. She may have no childcare experience. Her purpose for being in the country is to learn the language and culture. She should have a chance to attend school. Expect some difficulties in communicating your wishes if you don't speak the au pair's language.

Au pairs typically receive:
- a private room
- air fare
- $100.00 per week
- medical insurance
- up to $500.00 toward education

Eight au pair agencies have met federal guidelines. For a fee they screen applicants and match them with families. But try to choose your au pair yourself, from a group the agency selects. Find out from the candidates about their childcare experience and why they want to come to North America. Make sure the agency will replace your au pair if she doesn't work out. The United States Information Agency (USIA) will provide you with a list of the approved agencies (see Resources).

Childcare Centers

A childcare center is a business that provides childcare. It is housed in a building designed for the needs of small children. It may be run by a trained or untrained staff. Their aim is to give babies and children a secure and stimulating place in which to grow and develop. You can place your child in a childcare center if she is between birth and 5 years old. Childcare centers have set opening and closing times. They might cost $75.00 to more than $175.00 per week.

Workplace childcare centers are designed for the employees of an organization. The cost of care will often, but not always, be subsidized by the sponsoring company.

Mother's Helper

A mother's helper may have no formal training. You could expect her to run errands, help with the house and provide childcare.

A mother's helper may come from a foreign country. She may live in the home or out. Provide a list of the duties you expect the mother's helper to perform. Also, provide a clear-cut schedule of the hours you expect her to work. Whether she lives in or out, expect to pay the minimum wage allowed for the hours she works. You must also pay all payroll taxes.

Health Concerns

You don't want to hire an in-home worker who can pass a serious disease to you or your child. In-home workers should be tested for tuberculosis, and possibly for other diseases as well. Foreign workers may have been exposed to diseases that are less common in the United States and Canada.

What Can You Afford?

Once you know what you can choose from, you need to see what you can afford. Is childcare going to come out of one or two salaries? What will your salary be when you return to work? The same? Or will you be working fewer hours now and earning less? Is there a workplace childcare center?

If you hire a nanny, you are her employer. Therefore you will have to pay payroll taxes on top of her net salary. Be sure to add in that amount when you figure out what you can afford. In the United States, you should add about 20% of the net salary or so, for payroll taxes. You must pay these taxes each quarter, and use the right forms. The payroll taxes you must pay in the United States include: (a) federal income tax; (b) social security (FICA); (c) Medicare; (d) state disability insurance (SDI); and (e) state income tax (in some states). In Canada, expect to contribute to your employee's pension and her employment insurance (EI). You will also pay income tax and insure your household for workman's compensation.You might want to hire a payroll service or an accountant to help you get started.

If you have more than one child and are going back to work, what is the most cost-effective method of childcare? Check whether your options offer discounts for more than one child.

Think broadly about the ramifications of your choice. For example, an au pair may be the cheapest form of childcare. But she may not have experience in infant care. So although it would be cheap, this option may not be best for you and your family.

Distance from Office or Home

You may want to consider the distances between your office, home and childcare. What is best for you? Should the childcare be closer to home or office?

If you are the one who will drop off and pick up your child, then maybe close to the office is best. But if your partner will be involved too, then childcare closer to home or his work may be better.

How old is your child or baby? If they have friends, then childcare close to home might give them the chance to visit with friends. But, if you are still breastfeeding, it might make more sense to find childcare close to the office. See chapter 11 for more on breastfeeding and working.

Do You Want Household Help Too?

This decision could alter the choice of caregiver. A sitter is not likely to give you a hand with the house. Many nannies would do the children's washing and cleaning, but not yours. An au pair could do "light housework" and so on.

This may be the time to think about how you run your household. Your free time with your family will become even more precious. So maybe you could get someone to clean once a week. This could be something else to include in your budget.

A Caregiver to Fit Your Workstyle

How will you be working?

If you are working from home, would you rather your child was cared for out of the house all the time? This might keep you from (a) taking over if the child is upset, which could undermine your caregiver, or (b) letting your child disrupt your work. Or would you prefer to have the child close by? Then you could have lunch together and so on.

You may need a different type of care if you work part-time or full-time. Some childcare centers, with waiting lists, only offer full-time places. Or they may have certain part-time options, but these may be too limiting. Some caregivers prefer not to pick up after school. At the end of the school day, children are often tired and may be cranky.

Night work brings its own issues. If you are a couple, then your partner may be home at night to take over the childcare. This is a good, inexpensive option. But you may pay a high price in terms of your relationship. You may see very little of each other.

If you are a single parent working at night, this may not be an option. Could you take the child with you? Some hospitals, and a growing number of companies, now provide 24-hour childcare. Otherwise you would need to get a sitter to come to your home. Other childcare centers will be closed.

Childcare before 9:00 am and after 5:00 pm

The workplace is moving toward a service-based economy. Service jobs have the highest and fastest-growing percentage of shift workers (42%). Many services operate during early mornings, nights and weekends. Many of these jobs are held by women.

In 1990, 7.2-million mothers with 11.7 children under age 15 worked either full- or part-time during nonstandard hours.

Source: Children Today, Fall-Winter 1995, v23, n4, page 8.

Types of Nonstandard Childcare

1. Single Employer
   The Toyota Corporation built a 24-hour Child Development Center at its Georgetown, Kentucky, plant. It is licensed for 230 children, from 6 weeks to 13 years of age.

   In Boston, the Massachusetts Bay Transit Authority (MBTA) has a Reserved Slot Childcare Program. Employees' children between 2 months and 12 years of age may receive care under contract with 32 licensed childcare centers. These centers are located in 23 different communities.

2. Employer Consortium
   Some companies join together to provide childcare for employees. In Atlanta, Georgia, the Marriott, OMNI and Hyatt Hotels joined to create the Children's Inn of Atlanta. It provides service to families of low-income hotel workers, including childcare. Its early-learning center for 250 children is open 24 hours a day, 7 days a week.

3. Community Partnership
   In Burlingame, California, the Palcare Childcare Center was created by unions, employers and local governments. It serves children from 3 months to 5 years of age, whose parent works at the San Francisco International Airport. It is open 24 hours a day, 7 days a week.

Access to a Car

If you have a car, you can choose any kind of childcare you can afford. If you don't have a car, you might want to think about having a sitter come to your house.

If transportation is a problem, you might need to do some creative thinking. What about neighbors? Could you persuade a neighbor to care for your child? Are there any retired people living nearby who might like to earn some extra money? What about older teenagers? Some may have younger brothers and sisters that they're used to caring for. And their own parents may be close by to give back-up support, if needed.

Is there an elementary school close by? Sometimes they will know people living nearby who can look after children. What about local churches or temples? Can they refer you to someone? Is a mother-and-toddler group part of the church or temple? Maybe you could start going for a while. A mother from the group may be able to help. By asking enough people, you may find some help.

Sometimes help comes from strange sources. So let people know what your needs are, and see if there is any response. Talk to your neighbors about this. It's a good way to get to know them. Even if they can't help you, the contacts you make can only be good. Your neighbors may become your friends.

Think about your key needs, such as those above. Talk to people who have solved the same problems. What did they do?

Hard Times

This can be a hard time for parents. Just when you think you are coping with parenthood and its stresses you are faced with even more decisions. You may lack confidence at first. You may not know what is best for your child. You may not be sure you want to return to work. And you may not be ready to choose who will be right to look after your child. Keep your options open. If the childcare center you wanted is full, don't be upset. You will find the right place.

Remember, circumstances can change. Nothing is set in stone. You may not want to make changes. But it is far better to do that, and make both you and the child happier, than to put up with a mistake to prevent an upset.

First of all, give yourself time. You might find the right person quickly. But it may also take a while. It helps if you can be flexible. Don't feel you are being backed against a wall.

CHECKLIST

Checklist of people to contact

1. Local Social Service department for lists of childcare centers.

2. National Association of Child Care Resource and Referral Agencies (see Appendix).

3. Local domestic agencies for nannies, au pairs, mother's helpers.

4. Local colleges with childcare courses. Place ads for nannies.

5. Personnel department of your or your partner's company. Learn about maternity-leave policies and workplace childcare, if any.

6. Local churches, temples or community groups—are there support groups for working mothers? If not, can you help start one?

7. Your child's doctor may be able to suggest babysitters or other childcare options.

You need time to try your options. Find out what they are really like. Do a few test runs. Some plans don't work right away. But you may see ways to improve them with time. Sometimes you'll know you made a mistake. Then you need to change your plans. Try to give yourself enough time to do this before you go back to work. It takes a lot of pressure off. Once you have found the right place for your child, you can relax. Let your child go there for a few hours a week. Then slowly build up to the big moment, when he or she will stay all day.

Start your search by calling agencies or Social Service departments. Place ads in the local paper. Talk on the phone to narrow your list. Then begin to interview candidates.

Questions to Ask Yourself

Start a list of things that you want from childcare. This will help you sort out the best option for you. Here are a few things that you might think about:

- Do you want someone whose lifestyle is like yours? Or would you prefer someone who might offer a contrast? For example:
  "I wanted my sitter to have a different lifestyle, so my children would look forward to the contrast. Our sitter had lots of animals. She used to take Jamie to the livestock show."
- Do you want someone with the same sort of beliefs as yours, so you can relate to them? What about any religious preference?
- Do you want someone to clean up while you are at work?
- Will you be sending one child or more? Do they have the same needs?
- Do you want someone young and lively? Or would you prefer someone more mature?
- Do you want a male or a female caregiver? One of the mothers interviewed sent her child to a workplace childcare center where her main caregiver was a male. It worked very well. There are also some husband-and-wife childcare teams.
- Food: Do you want to supply it? Or are you happy to let someone else do it?
- Are you organized in the morning?
- Do you want your child to be with other children? Or would you prefer one-to-one care?

- Do you want an active, child-centered schedule? Or would you prefer a home-like setting, where your child fits in with the daily routine of the caregiver? Your child might go shopping with her, pick up other children from school, and so on.
- How flexible do you need your caregiver to be?
- Do their feelings about breastfeeding or feeding a baby with expressed breast milk matter to you? *"I preferred to have a nanny at home. I was breastfeeding. I didn't want to express milk and take it to the childcare center. I feel there's a fine line between being a great, wholesome mother and feeling like a complete fool in front of someone else. If you're breastfeeding, you're not objective. The idea that somebody might find expressed breastmilk repulsive is strange to you."*
- Do you want someone who will also babysit for you at night?
- Does your partner need to get along with the caregiver too?
- Are you worried that there may be a clash of wills if your child is left alone with her caregiver?

Contact as many groups and people as you can. This will give you the broadest view of options. Talk to other parents. Find out what sort of questions they asked. Make a list or a chart. Then you can begin to see a pattern emerge of your preferred type of childcare.

Important factors	Workplace	Nursery	Caregiver	Nanny
Close to me	✔			
Making local friends		✔	✔	
Family setting			✔	✔
Can leave EBM (expressed breast milk)			✔	✔
Can babysit				✔

The Interview and Your Selection

You will find more about how to interview and what questions to ask in chapter 8. But here we look at the broad issues of the interview and your selection.

Many people have never chosen someone to work for them before. Their job may not involve hiring new staff members. They have never needed a housekeeper, a gardener or anyone else to work around the house.

Selection

Once you have learned what types of care there are, how do you decide whether you want to go any further with them? You need to have a short list of points that must be met before you can proceed. What matters most to you? This list will be personal. Your list may include: distance from home, how many other children there are, or if the caregiver smokes. Think about what you want from your caregiver. Then it will be easier to cross off those who don't fit your needs. Don't feel guilty about rejecting people. It's just part of the process.

If you advertise, you may get responses by phone. Keep index cards by the phone to fill in details when people call. Have a list of key questions ready to ask.

Domestic agencies deal with nannies, mother's helpers, au pairs and so on. They should be able to make the selection for you. If you do employ an agency, make sure they do the work! For example, make sure they have current contact with the candidate. Maybe she was a good match two years ago, but the agency should check to make sure her capabilities are still the same.

Be specific about what you want. If they start sending you resumes of people who don't fit your needs, they should have a very good reason for doing so, or they should stop. If they don't, use another agency. You can be choosy!

Interviews

In the interview, don't forget to:
1. Plan where you will hold the interview
2. Make a list of topics and key questions you want to cover
3. Ask open questions
4. Listen to the candidate's replies. What is she *not* saying?

Amy says: *"The best-qualified person is not always the best person for the job. Some people have natural skills. The best nanny I had wasn't trained at all. She started caring for three of my children when she was 17 years old."*

What do you want to find out? Lots of people feel awkward asking questions. Alex did too. But she knew it was a means to an end and got used to it: *"I felt awkward at first, asking questions. I lost my fears when I saw the questions prompted very revealing answers. I learned things I wouldn't have learned otherwise."*

It's also good to notice what the candidate asks *you*. That can be a good guide to her values. She should ask you, first, about your children, their likes and dislikes, rather than how much you will pay her!

Where are you giving the interview? If you are choosing a family day-care home, it's not just the person but her house that you are "interviewing." Is it clean? Is it safe? How much space can the children use? Does it have a yard? Ria chose someone whose house was clean but a little messy, with lots of toys out. What are the other children or her own children like? If that matters to you, ask if you can visit her when they are present. Don't be surprised if she'd rather you not visit after school, when all the children are tired.

Contracts

It's good to agree to a contract when you make arrangements with any kind of caregiver for your child. You can include all the points that you and the caregiver have discussed. Then it becomes a useful document to which you can refer if you ever disagree about terms. It can be as simple or as complex as you like. But it should include salary, how much notice you agree to give each other, hours, vacations and holidays. There is a sample contract for a nanny on pages 123-124, which is detailed. It shows some items you might want to include.

You and the caregiver may want to draw up the contract together, so you are both happy with the terms.

Sharing the Risks and Duties

When you place your child with a caregiver, you share duties and expose your child to new risks. This can evoke feelings of guilt in a parent. But with time and a caregiver you trust, all parties can benefit.

Sarah talks about how she felt: *"Before I had Lucy, I didn't think about the guilt, the questioning and feeling torn. Lucy settled into childcare just fine. But I wondered what went on in her mind, even though on the surface things were OK. It got easier, but it took longer than a couple of weeks. I never felt totally at ease. Like lots of other things about children, it's never clear-cut. I always felt uncertain. As the parent, you're the one who's responsible. I found being a parent hard to get used to."*

Many parents feel very protective towards their children. This can make choosing a caregiver hard. You may ask yourself why you are leaving your child, how can you leave your child, and so on. There may be times you feel you cannot bear to leave him in someone else's care. If that feeling prevails, perhaps you could choose another option. Most parents feel like this at some point, so it is worth telling yourself you are not deserting your children when you find good-quality childcare for them.

Precautions

- Ask for and contact at least two references.
- Ask around. A bad caregiver can become "known" to other parents. Do a trial run of a few hours a week before making your final decision.
- In California, contact Trustline, at 1-800-822-8490, for a free background check of unlicensed childcare workers.
- In the United States, local police or sheriff departments can check for prior arrests or convictions for child or sexual abuse. This service is free, but it is provided at the discretion of each local law-enforcement agency. (It is called "Megan's Law".)
- Draw up a contract.
- Trust your instincts.
- Include a trial period. Then have a meeting with your childcare provider to discuss how things are going.

In the United States in 1996, only four states required licensed childcare providers to be fingerprinted and checked for criminal arrests and convictions.

How can you be sure that your caregiver can be trusted? What if something happened and your child was injured in some way? It would be untrue to say this never happens. Sometimes you read in the newspapers that a childcare worker has injured or abused a child in her care. Clearly, in these cases the wrong people are doing the wrong job. Or there might have been an accident.

Part of being a good parent means doing the best possible thing for your child. We can take precautions. But if you have a gut instinct that someone is not right for you, don't leave the child there, even if it's the last option.

Warning Signs of Possible Physical or Sexual Abuse

Most childcare workers are trustworthy people. But a few are not fit to care for children. You may not always be able to tell the difference. The warning signs below may point to a possible problem with your child's care. Don't jump to conclusions. But look into the reasons for any of the following:

* Sudden dislike of or reluctance to go to caregiver.
* Sudden sexual acting out (sexual language, enactment of sex acts, including oral sex).
* Sudden hesitation over showing or receiving affection.
* Sudden sleep problems (nightmares, fear of dark or being alone).
* Regression to baby behaviors (bedwetting, thumbsucking, clinginess).
* Unusually nervous or aggressive behavior.
* Caregiver or center does not welcome your unannounced visits.
* Caregiver or center does not willingly provide the names and numbers of other parents who have children enrolled.
* Bruises, swollen areas, lacerations or other marks.
* Implausible explanations by child or caregiver regarding injuries.
* Anything your child says regarding physically or sexually abusive or inappropriate behavior.

Source: Clinical Reference Systems, Dec. 1994, page 1185

Remember that all preschools and childcare centers should be licensed. If they are not, don't place your child there. If family day-care homes are licensed in your state or province, only use a licensed home. Nannies don't have to be licensed. But you could spend time at home after the nanny starts, so you can build a trusting relationship. Any good nanny will understand why you need to do this. Once you have returned to work, enlist support of nonworking friends. Get them to drop by without notice to see what's happening. That can reassure you.

Crime programs on TV often end with the announcer saying in effect, "Don't have nightmares. These crimes are very rare." This may be true. But you have to be happy yourself with your caregiver. If not, you will never be able to leave your child behind. And if you do, your thoughts will stay with your child, instead of on your work.

Chapter 6

Family Day-Care Homes

In many states and most provinces, family day-care homes must be licensed. An official will inspect the home to ensure:
- there are no safety hazards
- there is enough space for children to play in
- the home is properly equipped

Many states and provinces require a course of study for the childcare worker before a home may be licensed. This may include topics such as:
- first aid
- home safety
- environmental health
- child development and play
- child-protection issues
- equal opportunities
- the business side of childcare work
- partnership with parents

Caregivers with licensed family day-care homes are self-employed. They should also be insured in case an accident happens while a child is in their care.

Those who run family day-care homes are often mothers themselves. Most of the time, this is the way they have gained their experience. For some parents, it is this knowledge of raising a family that makes a family day-care home an appealing choice. As Alex says, *"A television program I saw made me feel very doubtful about preschool care. My baby was only going to be 3 months old when I went back to work. I felt a family atmosphere was right for her. Even though I wouldn't be there, she would be in the same kind of place she would be if I were at home with her."*

When a family day-care home is licensed, a limit is set on the ages and number of children who may receive care there. This limit varies by state and province.

The Benefits

Extended Family

Cassie found that Ian had made strong bonds with the caregiver's children, and the other children who went there too. *"My son was 7 months old when he started going to family day care. He stopped when he was 2-1/2 years old. The caregiver's children became like brothers and sisters to him. He was very much a baby brother to them. He missed them badly when he stopped going there."* The advantage of the second family is clear. But Cassie regrets not thinking about the timing more when she herself decided to give up work. She now wishes she had waited until Ian was old enough to go to a playgroup, so he could make new friends quickly.

For Alex, and many others, one of the attractions of a family day-care home is that their child is being cared for in a home. There are other benefits, too.

Another Mother Figure

Not only do children get other playmates, but they also gain a second mother figure to care for them while their own parents are at work. Kari's daughter, Jo, goes to a family day-care home. Kari describes their relationship: *"Basically she loves Jo. They love one another. She treats her as the third child she never had."*

Kari finds the relationship supportive beyond their mutual commitment to Jo. *"She's my alter ego during the day. I get mail-order packages delivered to her house. If I need to change times or days on short notice, she will always try and take Jo if she can. She's pretty flexible. She's got my front-door key because I've locked myself out twice already."*

Nonstandard Hours

Having a job that doesn't follow normal hours sometimes makes it hard to get "official" childcare. Lucy is a training consultant. She may work for two very long days, but then be home for a week. *"My parents would drive down from their home the day before the course started. They'd stay till it was over. But it was a long way to come each time. I didn't think of a family day-care home at first because I had been told that they only work certain hours. That made sense to me, because they have their own families to attend to. But then I found out some family day-care homes are very flexible. It depends on their own circumstances. So from then on that's what I did."*

Flexible Care

One factor that concerns many women is how flexible their childcare can be. Of course, there has to be a regular commitment to the caregiver. But some people find that a schedule that has to be made well in advance, or one that requires the same hours each day, is not the way they work.

Using a family day-care home can solve some of these problems. Such a home may take your child full-time or part-time, as Sylvette found. And they will often be flexible about hours. *"I started looking for childcare when Emma was 2 or 3 months old. I had been thinking about the options and had read a lot about it. I felt from what I read that a family day-care home would be best for me. I wasn't sure of the hours I'd need because I was starting to take college classes. I knew I needed flexible childcare. I understood from the*

preschools I visited that I would have to commit to a certain number of days per week. And I would have to pay for that all year. Another concern about preschools was I felt there could be a high staff turnover.

"I didn't want a nanny. They cost too much. And most nannies haven't had children. But people who run a family day-care home usually have.

"Sometimes you have to trust your own feelings and that 'gut instinct.' I didn't have any luck finding a family day-care home in my town. I found the whole process very tough. I didn't like having to ask personal questions. So I contacted the National Association of Child Care Resource and Referral Agencies, in Washington, D.C. They put me in touch with a referral agency in my area. That agency suggested a nearby town that had some good family day-care homes. I had a positive result from that. I was happy with the first family day-care home I visited. Why was I happy with this one? I guess it's an instinct. You know when it feels right."

Cost

Rates vary greatly by area and demand. But often family day-care homes are the least costly form of childcare. The only cheaper form of care is to use a member of your family or a friend who doesn't charge. Part-time places that bill on an hourly rate often cost more than full-time places.

Experience That Counts ...

A caregiver in a family day-care home has a strong advantage over other caregivers. They often have families of their own. Some parents find this experience of mothering a great comfort. This may be of greatest help with a first child, when a new mother may not know what to do at times.

Laura valued the expertise of her caregiver: *"I had no problems leaving my little girl there. I had an excellent caregiver. She showed me how to do things I thought I was no good at."*

If you are a first-time parent you might feel better leaving your child with a caregiver who has had children herself. If you see the caregiver's children are happy and well cared for, you may feel better about leaving your own child with her.

Standards

If a family day-care home is licensed, it should have been checked for safety. It is not likely that a licensed home and caregiver would accept more children than the limit prescribed by law.

Problems

- Some children feel more secure in their own home. They don't want to leave their own home each day.
- Going to a family day-care home may restrict a child's social life. This can become a problem as they get older.

Older children may find going to a family day-care home restrictive, as Vanessa and Beth, aged 14 and 12, point out: *"When we've been to school all day, we'd like to come back to our own house and have something to eat, just like an adult. If you go to a day-care home, it can be boring if no other children are there. And you can't have your friends to your own house until later.*

"Children's feelings matter too. They've had a hard day too and want to come home and relax."

- Children are likely to pick up more colds, bugs and so on if they are outside their own home, mixing with other children.
- A less-than-perfect caregiver may favor her own children over your child.
- You have less control over how your child spends her time. The TV may be on longer than you'd like. Or perhaps there is a stash of toy guns you had sworn your child would never play with.
- If the caregiver is sick, you could be left on your own. Some caregivers have their own support network and will help each other out in times of sickness. But this isn't always the case.
- If you take your child to a family day-care home, you are the one doing the driving around. Your trip to and from work will be lengthened.
- If your child doesn't get along with the caregiver for some reason, you may have to make a complete change.
- There may be a clash between your children and the caregiver's children.

Arguments among children can be very hard for the children involved. If the clash is with the child of the caregiver, it can be a real problem. The other child may claim the higher ground because it is his or her own house. What can be done about this?

Joan was surprised when her school-age daughter, Lauren, didn't get along with the caregiver's child: *"I was looking for someone who would get along with James, because he is the youngest. He hadn't been in childcare before. Diana takes care of Lauren as well. There are problems there because her daughter is in Lauren's class and they don't get along. I took it for granted there wouldn't be any issues with Lauren, because she was the older one."* Joan listened to her daughter. She tried to explain that for Lauren, this form of childcare would only last for 3 months, while she was taking training classes for her job. She treated her as a rational person. Lauren understood and accepted the short-term nature of the problem.

Each person has their own perspective when looking for the right family day-care home.

Kari felt lucky. *"I dreaded the prospect of looking for childcare. I didn't know how I was going to interview people about caring for my child. How could I make such an important decision on the basis of a couple of hours? I didn't know how I was going to cope with it.*

"But when Dee, the woman who did my cleaning, offered to do it, I felt it was the perfect answer. We knew her family, too. I couldn't believe my luck. She took some training and became licensed as a family day-care home. I felt that was better for both of us. She gave up her part-time job, which she hated. She was delighted to stay at home and do what she had always wanted to do.

"Dee's boys were five and three. She cared for one other girl now and then, and only Jo full-time. Dee takes Jo to the gym and for swimming lessons. It's like having a nanny. Jo has this secret circle of friends I have never met. But I feel I know them well. It's such a relief to me. I have absolute trust in Dee. The only time I feel guilty is when Jo is ill. If she's under the weather, Dee is happy to take her. She will even take her to the doctor for me. But I feel bad because she would rather be with me. At least, I think so!

"Sometimes Jo will call me Dee and Dee mommy. They all do that, don't they? But she calls here home, and Dee's house is Dee's. I'd be more concerned if someone was in our house and she had two mother figures in the same house.

"Nothing's perfect, of course. Jo can't go to the preschool I prefer because it's out of town. Dee doesn't drive. So she goes to one next to her boys' school.

"I pay Dee for vacations and holidays, even though I don't have to. But I feel I'm getting Cadillac service. This really works."

For Sally, things didn't go so well. *"I went back to work when Hannah was 22 weeks old. My leave was 18 weeks, but I wasn't quite ready then. My employers were flexible. So I stayed at home an extra four weeks.*

"I had found someone to take care of Hannah. But Hannah wouldn't take a bottle. She also wouldn't go to other people too well. What I also learned later was that although this lady had a family day-care home, she had very little experience with babies. Hannah cried all day. At the end of the first day, the caregiver said she couldn't cope. I had to find someone else.

"Luckily, by the end of the second week I did find someone else. I talked to a lot of my friends to see if they knew of anyone. And I did find the right person. She was a hospital-nursery nurse. She was prepared to come to my

house for the two full days that I need her. I also work on a third day. But my husband, who works a 4-day week, takes care of Hannah that day."

Barbara had a bumpy start to her childcare plans too. *"Mark is in his second family day-care home now. I went back to work when he was 4 months old. I'd gotten a family day-care home lined up in advance. He started going there before I was back at work. And about two weeks before I was due back I noticed a strong smell each time I went to the house to pick him up. One day I went to the kitchen and saw a hamster's cage right next to the baby's bottles. That was it. I paid her fully and took him out of there.*

"I was distraught. Two weeks to go and no childcare! I looked in a local paper, which covered the area close to my office. I found an ad for someone who had just gotten her home licensed for family day care. When I went to see her we got along very well. And because she was new, she had no hard-and-fast rules. She just said we could sit down and discuss working together for Mark.

"Now Mark is one of the family. Her youngest child is 10, so Mark is the baby. He had one-to-one care for the first 18 months. Then Karen took another toddler. Now he has someone to play with.

"One incident made me stop and think, though. I was there one day when he hurt himself badly enough to need a hug. He went straight to Karen. It didn't really worry me, because he was so settled there. But Karen was embarrassed."

Whatever kind of childcare you go for, there is a strong chance that your child will form an attachment to one person. It's more likely to happen with a nanny or a family day-care caregiver than in a preschool. But it is common to hear children confuse names. They might call the caregiver mommy and call mommy by the caregiver's name. Many mothers don't like it when someone else is so close to their child. But it means that your child feels secure when he's with that person. If you know your child feels secure, you can feel more relaxed about leaving him while you work.

Sue found it was hard to find a caregiver who would care for a baby. Her daughter Alexa was 4-1/2 months old at the time. *"They have to really want babies, because babies are hard work. Another thing I was aware of is that it's not just the caregivers you interview and question. It's their houses, big or small, yards, space, use of rooms. And, most of all, it's their standards."*

When Rita looked for a family day-care home, she didn't want ones that were too clean and tidy. She wanted her children to have free access to toys and playthings. She also chose a caregiver who had four children of her own. She was clearly going for experience and a family environment. *"For Becky, this was another family. I didn't have any guilty feelings. I knew that Becky was happy there. This was where she chose to go when I went into labor with our second child."*

View from Family Day-Care Homes

Lots of women who become licensed to provide family day care do so because they want or need to work. But they are not happy leaving their children. A morning spent discussing the role of a family day-care home with a group of caregivers revealed a great deal.

Reasons for becoming licensed to provide family day care vary: *"Because I like being with children." "Because I don't want to leave my children to go to work." "Because my partner/husband doesn't want me to work outside the home." "I needed the money."*

Most family day-care homes don't take babies younger than 6 months old. But there is a growing trend among working mothers to feel that they can leave them earlier than that. It is important for a caregiver to feel that they can make a strong bond with the child. They are making a long-term commitment to him or her.

Wendy is now a grandmother. But she still enjoys running a family day-care home. She cared for brothers who are now 11 and 13. Now she is looking after their younger brother. *"We are ideal for each other. This mother is not the maternal type, and I am. I'm not being critical. It's just the way things are. We both enjoy doing what we do."*

Benefits

Many of the caregivers felt there were plenty of good points about family day care—for themselves, the children and the parents.

"Mothers can return to work. They know their children have lots of stimulation from other children."

"A caregiver in family day care doesn't get bothered by having children around. We enjoy them. We want to do lots of things with them. We will take them out to the park. When you've got lots of kids, you want to keep them happy."

"We, as caregivers, benefit too. Our children have instant companions. They miss them when the others aren't around."

Problems

Sometimes there can be problems. Most problems come up when parents and caregivers differ about discipline.

"I have felt with some parents that we differ over treatment of behavior. I cared for a little girl who was fine with me all day. But then, when her mother picked her up, she would be dreadful. I would tell the mother this, but her mother would give her presents. I felt that was rewarding the bad behavior. But I can say nothing about it. It makes my job tougher. I also feel that it undermines me with the child."

"One parent told me she never says 'no' to her child. She just distracts him. But I have to say 'no' to my children. I found it very hard to do what she wanted. I couldn't treat her child one way and my own children another. If they were all doing something naughty, how could I not say 'no' to just one of them? But I talked to her about it. In the end she accepted that I had to treat her child the same way I did mine."

"If a parent has a problem with something, I think you need to talk about it at the start."

One of the biggest childcare issues is whether to spank or not. The view in this group seemed to be totally against spanking. There were comments such as: *"I'm not going down that road, even though some mothers tell me to;" "As a mother, I wouldn't spank my own children."*

Another place where parents and caregivers can sometimes disagree is food. As a parent it is best to be flexible about what your child eats. Of course, there may be special needs or restrictions.

"I would go along with the mother's feeding requests. But sometimes it can be hard on all of us. One mother brings her child's lunch each day. This causes problems because her child sees what my children are eating. Then she wants to eat that too. So I end up having to feed them at different times."

"A first-time mother may be horrified at the thought of her child going to McDonald's. But what if I want to take my 6-year-old there for lunch one day? I did that once. And the mother gave me a pasta-and-bean salad for her child to eat. I gave it to her. But I'm not sure if it was fair to her. I don't think there's an easy answer."

The group agreed that the greatest worry is for the child's safety. *"I worry about a child hurting herself while I'm caring for her. It would be terrible to have to tell the mother or father. We all know these things do happen. But I'd feel awful in case the parents thought I wasn't being watchful."*

Although more and more children are starting in family day care at younger ages, there can still be problems with the "clingy" stage. This tends to occur at around nine months. *"Often if they start early, they settle down very well. Sometimes they take longer to settle back down after vacations and holidays."*

Some suggestions for improving the child's chance of settling down: *"Get them to come in for a couple of hour-long visits." "Build up slowly, with short visits together at first. Then leave for 20 minutes at first and build up." "Get the fathers to come too. It helps if the whole family knows who's caring for the children."*

These caregivers felt strongly that finding the right family day-care home really matters. It is worth taking time to find the right one. Your child will be fitting into their way of life. Your lifestyles may differ in many respects. But your values should be similar.

A Few Points for Parents to Remember

Sometimes the extended-family concept can cause problems. There are benefits to any child being in a home where she is treated as one of the family. But this is, after all, a job for the caregiver. They will be more likely to remain flexible and respect you if you:

1. Agree to a payment schedule and stick to it.
2. Pick up the children on time. Problems do come up. But if you are late, pay extra. Don't assume it's just OK.
3. Give plenty of warning about changes of plans. This commitment is not just between you and the caregiver, it's to the child, too. If you do need to change family day-care homes, children survive. But try to make the transition as smooth as you can for them.
4. Think before you speak. Deirdre plans informational meetings on behalf of a group of women who run family day-care homes. She has to bite her tongue sometimes when asked questions like: "Do you have any well-educated caregivers?" But she feels that mostly people are all pulling in the same direction. She feels that there is no invasion of privacy when asked questions. But of course it depends on how they're asked.

5. If you disagree with the caregiver, you might want to talk about it right away. But it may be better to wait for a chance to call at night. Then little ears don't get a chance to hear too much. A child could play one person against the other, if she heard critical remarks.

6. Sometimes first-time mothers can feel undermined by a confident, experienced caregiver. There are benefits to experience. But a new mother may need time to feel her way. She doesn't want someone to tell her how it's done. Spend time to find someone who respects you and your opinions. She will be a person with whom you will be happy to leave your children.

The last word should go to the client on the receiving end of the childcare. Matt went to a family day-care home for after-school care once he started school. He had been at a preschool since he was a few months old, until he entered school. Both of his parents worked in Chicago when he started school. He is now 15: *"It didn't really bother me to go to family day care. I knew that my parents had to work. There was no other choice. I felt secure because I knew I would be picked up each night. Plus there were other children there to play with. You can't have friends over for a snack. But you do have kids there all the time to play with, which makes up for it."*

Finding a Family Day-Care Home

- Contact your local Social Services department. They may refer you to locally licensed family day-care homes. Then you can make your own choice. Sometimes there will be one contact who will suggest people near you with a vacancy. But often, you need to contact people directly.
- Ask other mothers if they know of a good family day-care home.
- Call up a few of the referred homes. Have a chat with the caregivers. This gives you a good start and may help you narrow the field immediately.
- Decide what matters most to you and what questions to ask.
- Visit a few family day-care homes. Meet the caregivers. But don't make a final decision until all interviews are over.
- Go back and discuss details with the caregiver at the family day-care

home you choose. You will need to agree on:
- hours
- rate of pay
- type of payment
- details about food consumption
- notice of changes
- time of drop-off and pickup
- who provides diapers, creams, diaper pails
- anything else that you want to agree about in advance

- Draw up a contract between you. Then you have something in writing to refer to if you don't agree on something.
- Agree to a verbal or written contract.
- Insist on seeing the original family day-care license and insurance certificate. Make sure they are current before you leave your child there.

Chapter 7

Preschools and Workplace Childcare Centers

Preschools and workplace childcare centers provide the same type of care. However, they differ in how they are run, who uses them and who pays for them.

In a preschool, you can expect to pay the total cost. A preschool is open to the general public. A workplace childcare center is just for employees' children of one or more companies. Often a workplace childcare center is on site. Sometimes all or part of the cost of care is subsidized by the employers. Otherwise, both types of childcare are quite similar.

Benefits of Preschools or Childcare Centers

Stability

An established preschool is not likely to close. There is plenty of demand for good preschools. Although there may be staff turnover, the preschool will not change. Your child will go to the same place each day. For some, this is very comforting.

Stimulation

Preschools are child-centered. That doesn't mean nannies or other caregivers don't stimulate the children in their care. But in a preschool the focus is on the growth of childrens' and babies' skills. Preschools help children develop and they encourage social skills. Many parents who choose preschools do so for these reasons.

No Boring Chores

While other kinds of caregivers still have to do their own shopping and household chores, this isn't an issue in a preschool. Children at preschools find the day is geared to them, rather than when the dishes have to be done, for example.

Other Children

A woman I talked to runs three preschools. She told me: *"The children don't come here for the adults. They come here for the other children. That's how children learn, by watching and playing with other children."* A preschool provides playmates as well as a number of trained staff.

Open House

Talk to directors of preschools to find out what their approach is. Most are happy for parents to drop in at any time of day to see what's going on with the children. This can be comforting for the parents. They can see what happens at different times of the day. They get a chance to observe their child playing and relating with other children.

Better Hours

Preschools are not completely flexible, but most have improved their hours. Each school is different. The hours may not work for every family. Today, preschools are often open from 7:30 am to 6:00 or 6:30 pm. Some open even earlier.

Standards

Preschools may be inspected by the local Social Services department, which licenses them. This means they have minimum standards to uphold. These standards differ by state in the United States and by province in Canada. The standards cover issues such as safety, space for children and staff-child ratios.

Quality Control

When you send your baby or child to a preschool, you know they will be engaged in structured activities. They won't just play aimlessly with whatever is around. But not all preschools offer the same quality of care. Like other kinds of caregivers, some will appeal to one family but not to another. The director of a local preschool offered these tips for checking that a preschool provides quality care:

- The space itself should provide stimulation. The teacher or aide may not always be working with the children.
- Are there plenty of things to touch?
- Is the equipment treated with care by everyone?
- Is there free access to pencils, paper and other safe materials?
- Is the staff happy? Do they smile at you and your children?

Several Caregivers

Some parents prefer to be their child's prime caregiver. They want the child to see it that way, too. This means the thought of a sitter or a nanny is not as appealing as preschool care. At a childcare center or preschool, the caregivers are stable, but there isn't just one person or "mother figure" in the child's life.

Problems with a Preschool or Childcare Center

Hours

Although hours are improving, preschools and childcare centers are still not as flexible as other forms of childcare. You may drop off your child only after the childcare center is open, and pick him up before it has closed. If those hours don't suit you, you have no choice but to adapt or look for another situation. You could try to find a childcare center with longer hours. You could get a family day-care caregiver to pick up your child for you. Or you could choose another form of care.

Not for All Children

Some parents feel that a childcare center is not right for their child. It is a busy, active place. Children who are more timid might find it threatening. Amy sends her children to a childcare center, but not until they are two. She feels they belong at home until then. *"I do think that babies are better off at home until they are two. They do better in their own stable space, with which they are familiar."*

Competition

Some people think children in a preschool have to compete for attention more than they would at home. The question is, is that a bad thing? Is it even true?

Cost

Preschool care is one of the more expensive childcare options. There aren't often price breaks if you enroll more than one child.

Finding a Place

Childcare centers are often full, with waiting lists. It can be hard to find part-time places. Good places for infants can be even harder to find. You may need to sign up your child well in advance, maybe as soon as you find out you are pregnant. Childcare options can be a lot to think about when so much else is going on in your life.

Commitment

As in any other business, commitments need to be formalized. You may be asked to pay a deposit in advance to hold your child's place. Some childcare centers expect you to take vacations at the same time each year, when they are closed, or else pay for your child's place even though you are away.

Choices and Children

No one choice fits every child. Families' needs differ. Your best choice depends on all sorts of concerns, such as:

- What you can afford
- Your child's nature
- What your child likes
- What you want
- How many children you have

Karen manages three day-care centers. She spoke of her views on the preschool as a form of childcare: *"A good preschool is child-centered and runs at the child's pace. Our centers focus on the children. There are no household chores to be done. We take them to the park, to local stores, to mail letters. We try to make them feel part of the local community.*

"Preschool gives children an extended family. Being at home with mother for five years may not be enough. Children need more stimulation than a busy mother can often provide. They are happier with other friends than with adults. And if they have enough equipment to play with, they don't fight. Also, the staff is happy. They have their co-workers' support. They aren't isolated the way a mother or a nanny could be.

"There is a down side, of course. You still have to pay if your child is ill and doesn't attend. You still have to pay if you take vacations when the preschool is open. And it can become a bit rigid, because we have to have rules."

Karen had been a primary-grade schoolteacher before she set up her preschools. She felt children were starting school with untapped potential. *"Children absorb so much during those preschool years. They need stimulation. They learn from other children rather than adults. So we need to give them access to what they need to learn from."*

Karen has a flexible approach to getting children settled into childcare. She finds the younger they start, the sooner they adjust to life there. *"The difficult stage tends to be from two to three. But if they won't settle down and their mother wants to stay, that's fine. Sometimes having the parent stay just once gives the child more confidence.*

"When a child is upset here, we take them to watch a video, or take them for a walk in a stroller. It really depends on what happens to them in their own home.

"If a child is upset, you need to distract them. It gives them the chance to calm down and save face, if they're having a tantrum.

"We don't have a 'typical day.' But there are certain consistencies. We make sure everyone gets a turn with the equipment. We make sure all the equipment is out for them to play with. They also have a nap after lunch. Before they come to us we try to encourage parents to get them into a similar routine, with their naps at the same time."

Pat was able to make use of her company's workplace childcare. She comments: *"I always planned to return to work, unless there was something wrong with my baby. Happily, he was perfect. So I went back when he was 4 months old. My company was going through a transition, which included a move. The move was closer to home. Until that happened, my mother took Shawn three days a week.*

"A brand-new workplace childcare center was being built off-site. It was gorgeous. That was another thing that encouraged me to come back to work. It was close by in case of any problems. They served good food. There was a large yard for him to play in."

Laura's daughter, Holly, changed from going to a sitter to a workplace childcare center: *"My children started going to the office childcare center when Holly was 2-1/2 years old and Anna was 6 months old.*

"Holly had been with a sitter for two years. The change was difficult for her. She was OK if she stayed busy. Of course the childcare center is a stimulating place . . . but there were times when she was clingy and aggressive, which worried me. I wasn't happy about it. But I made the choice and I wanted to see it through.

"Even though it was hard for her, I felt the childcare center was the right place. I had faith in my employer that the care was good. And I had contact with other parents. I got a lot of positive feedback from them."

Holly did settle in after a while. Now she has started school. Laura says: *"Holly was in the childcare center four days a week for more than two years. She went into school very easily. I think that was thanks to the childcare center. Now she isn't daunted by large numbers of children."*

Julia's daughter Beth had started with a sitter. But she had to change to a part-time preschool. Julia explains: *"I arranged to go into work late for a month. That gave Beth time to get used to the preschool for two days a week. She still went to Anne, her sitter, for the other days. It was hard to drop her off because she didn't want to go in. She hated it. She would scream and hang on to me. She hated having her routine changed. She would say in the car, 'Where am I going today?' It got to the point where she became sick when she got there. How am I going to cope with this, I asked myself.*

"So I asked Anne if she would take her for the hour before preschool and then bring her to the school. She was happy to. In fact, when Anne took her, Beth was fine. Then we had a three-week vacation. When we came back, Anne was away. I had to take Beth for a week, and we were back to square one. I think she was really upset. But I tried hard not to appear tense about it.

"The next week, when Anne was back, Beth was very upset again. That upset Anne, who offered to take her back full-time. But I didn't want to change the routine again. I had given up her place at her playgroup. And I felt she should be mixing with other children. It wasn't the answer, for Anne to take her back full-time. Anyway, it didn't take long before she got settled. But it was awful till then!"

View from Childcare Centers

Emily works at a childcare center as a caregiver. She's been qualified for about a year. She likes working with the babies best. She gives us a taste of what it is like to spend a day at a childcare center. *"There are about 120 children and babies enrolled at the center. Only about 40 or 50 of them are full-time. The center is open from 7 am till 7 pm, but not many*

of the children are here that long. A full-time place for a baby is $285.00 a week.

"*What I like about it is the atmosphere and the company. If I were a nanny in a private home, I think I'd get bored. I'd miss having people to chat with during work.*

"*If the babies start here when they're under three months, they tend to settle in very well. At that age, they haven't gotten used to any other routine. If they come at four to six months, sometimes they cry when they are left. But what we see and what the parents see is very different. Most babies stop crying soon after the parent has gone. Once they're distracted, they stop. Very few keep crying and don't adjust. But sometimes it happens. I used to see one mother drop off her little boy, who was 5 months old. He would cry. And she would leave and sit in the parking lot and cry.*

"I try to distract them as quickly as possible. I don't want parents to feel guilty. I can imagine how it feels. It must really hurt. My job is to do my best for the children and the parents. I need to get along well with them.

"It can take one or two weeks for a baby to adjust. Often it's only the leaving that is hard. But some get upset when the other parents pick up their children.

"Some are fine at first, but as they get older they get more upset. Really, it's better if the parent leaves as soon as they can. If they leave quickly and wait outside the door they can hear the baby settle down. It only takes a few minutes to divert them.

"I feel children thrive in a childcare center. They can play all day, instead of waiting for Mom to play when she can. But it helps if the child is prepared for the change.

"We have a loose structure during the day. But the babies can drop off to sleep at any time. I can only think of one time when all the babies were asleep at the same time!

"When they come in, they have some breakfast. Then they sleep or play. At about 10:00, we do diaper changes all around. Then there's more sleep or play. And around 11:45 am, we clean up for lunch. Sometimes we take them out to the playground. There is a playroom if it's raining. The older children go outside for play and nature walks. We try to stick to the parents' routine as much as we can.

"At our childcare center, you can bring in your child for two trial mornings. On the first one, the parent stays. At the other one, the parent goes. That way, we all know what to expect. And people get to know faces.

"I do get attached to the children even though I shouldn't. It's not surprising. You have to like babies to do this job. What I really enjoy is seeing the babies develop and do things for the first time. Not only do we get fond of the babies, but they get fond of us too. I haven't met any yet that I didn't like."

Lisa is the assistant director in a small preschool. She said that more and more people want childcare for their babies from three months. They have a long waiting list for places. *"The younger the baby is, the easier it is for us to settle them in. But it also gets easier when they are older if they have been to a playgroup or are used to other children. Most children do settle in. I've been here for 2-1/2 years. Only one couldn't adjust. Sometimes a child just isn't ready. But waiting a month or two, if you can, can make all the difference.*

"Preschools need routines. You can't run one without them. This means a child will learn about rules very young—too young for some. On the other hand, we try to balance play and structure. That alone makes the transition to school a little easier.

"We combine free play, discussion time, talking about the weather, breaks for food and drinks, visits to the post office, the park (we have triple strollers) and structured play. We also have a playground outside."

What Should You Look for
When Choosing a Childcare Center?

- Plenty of qualified staff
- Signs of staff playing with the children
- Ask for their policies on discipline and behavior
- Lots of good, well-used equipment
- Signs that the children relate well to the staff
- Signs of lots of free time so children can learn to play with other children
- Ask to see the center's license and make sure it is current

Louise has nothing but praise for the childcare center her son went to. He was her first child. One benefit for her was he had plenty of company during the day. *"Luke went to a childcare center from nine months to 20 months. He was a happy child, and he settled in well. Since he was an only child at the time, I liked him playing with others when I was at work.*

"He was able to do things like painting and messy games. He wouldn't have done those things so young if he had been at home. But childcare centers are equipped to do these things, which I liked. You also know the children are going to be playing, rather than watching too much TV."

Finding a Childcare Center

The best way may be by word-of-mouth referral. Childcare centers and preschools must be licensed through Social Services in most states and provinces. You can contact these offices to learn about childcare centers near you. Or contact the National Association of Child Care Resource and Referral Agencies (see Resources).

Chapter 8

Nannies

A number of parents prefer childcare that enables their children to stay in their own home. They choose from: a live-in or -out nanny, a mother's helper, an au pair or even a baby sitter who prefers to go to the child's house.

A Nanny

Having a nanny is no longer only for the rich. It is now one of the most popular forms of childcare, along with having an au pair, which is discussed in chapter 9.

There are different kinds of nannies. There are elite, old-fashioned nannies and newly trained nannies of 19. A nanny who is not officially qualified should have a great deal of work experience. The choice is yours, of course. You may find someone through word of mouth who has no formal training or work experience, but is a natural with children.

A nanny is not likely to do any housework. Her job is to look after the children, on a "sole-charge" basis. This means the children are in her care while she is on duty. Many nannies do not like their employers to be around. It may create confusion about who is in charge. It's hard for a mother to ignore her child crying, and she may want to intervene. But really it is the nanny's job to deal with an issue like that. That way, her authority can't be undermined in the child's eyes.

Nannies may live in or outside the home. If she lives in, she may cost less in terms of salary, because she will also be receiving room and board. This is part of the package; you can't charge rent. That means you must have a home big enough for an extra person. She will need her own room, at least. It should be big enough for her to feel at ease in during her time off.

She may need use of a car, if she doesn't have one of her own, to take the children places, such as to friends' homes and play groups. This applies whether she lives in or out.

Cost

This depends on factors such as age, experience, location and hours worked. It ranges from about $200.00 to $400.00 or more per week, plus room and board. If you employ a nanny, expect to pay taxes on her salary. Figure them into your budget. (See page 64 for more information.) There are now firms who run a payroll system for nannies. They take all the figuring and the paperwork out of your hands.

Nanny agencies will supply you with likely costs in your area for the hours of service you need. Look in your local newspaper or the Yellow Pages.

Benefits of a Live-in Nanny

Warm Family Relations

When a nanny lives in the home, she can be treated either as an employee or as part of the family. Each family decides that for themselves. One benefit of a live-in nanny is that she is part of the home. She will get to know all the members of the family. She is there all the time for the child. The child will see her as part of the family and may feel more secure.

Staying In Your Own Home

This can make a child feel more secure. It may help reduce the number of colds, coughs and other bugs your child gets. Children who are cared for outside the family home are exposed to more kinds of germs. They may suffer from colds more frequently.

Nannies are often employed by working parents who have a lot of commuting to do. They may be out of the house from seven in the morning to seven at night. The benefits of the child being at home in that situation are obvious.

A More Relaxed Start

This aspect of having a nanny is a real winner! If the nanny is in the home, it means she can't be late for work. She is there, on the spot. Often she will be expected to start work at seven or eight o'clock in the morning. This leaves you time to get yourself ready without having to get the children washed, dressed and breakfasted too.

This arrangment also means you can spend more time with the children at leisure. You're not all rushing to get out of the door by a certain time. You can take time to talk to the children or cuddle the baby in the morning. If you have a nanny to take over for you, you can get yourself ready. Maybe you can even sit down to breakfast with the children before you go out the door. The nanny will wash and dress them after you have gone.

Babysitting Services

When you negotiate terms with a nanny, you may ask her to babysit as part of her duties, one or two nights a week. You may have to pay her extra for more than that.

In this case, you have a babysitter who knows your children well. A good sitter is one less person you have to find at short notice. It also means she can put the children to bed, which is a great bonus. Some parents feel they have to get the children tucked into bed and asleep before they can go out. Then they pray the kids don't wake before they come back! A nanny on hand for this service can ease the burden a great deal.

Cost Effective with More Children

You may pay a nanny more if you have more than one child. But it won't be double, unlike a nursery school. In fact, the more children you have, the more cost-effective a nanny may be.

Variety

If work experience matters a lot to you, you may choose an older nanny. But you may want someone who is young and lively, who wants to take the children swimming or to the playground. A young, single nanny may be a good choice, not only for your child but also for you and your privacy. She will probably have an active social life and want to be out for a lot of her spare time.

Some Help around the House

Although nannies would not expect to be asked to do most housework, you could have them take care of tasks that have to do with the children, such as:

- Wash and iron the children's clothes
- Keep the children's rooms tidy
- Plan, buy and prepare the children's food

One-on-One with the Children

Your children will likely form a strong bond with their nanny. They will miss out on having other children about. But they will have one person's complete attention. They won't have to compete for attention with a larger group of children. This is very much substitute parenting. It may not appeal to parents who feel it is good for children to become more independent and learn to share. But even if you employ a nanny, you can still send your children to playgroups or group lessons. But it will be the nanny, not you, who brings them back and forth.

Problems with a Live-in Nanny

Personality Clashes

This is more likely to happen if someone comes into your home each day. Things may seem to be going well. But then you don't see eye to eye on something and a rift develops. You will have to think carefully about this when you interview your candidates. Try to find out as much as you can about their habits and preferences.

If there is a clash, talk about it as soon as possible. Otherwise an awkward moment can quickly become an impossible situation. Be direct and pleasant—that's important. You will need all your diplomatic skills. Unless you feel there is a fundamental problem, it is worth finding a solution rather than risk losing your caregiver and a good companion for your child.

Always Around

In many ways it is great to have someone around all the time. But it can also impose on your private life. It may take getting used to. And it is certainly one of the factors to weigh when you decide if you want someone to live in.

Behavior Problems

This is a sensitive issue. Where do you draw the line between someone making herself at home and cleaning out the cupboard of your peanuts or chocolates or white wine week after week? Or spending most of her spare time on the telephone? Be sure to set ground rules from the beginning.

No Children of Her Own

A young nanny is not likely to have had children of her own. Some parents find this a problem. They feel childcare courses are no substitute for the real thing. A nanny may not understand what it is like to leave your child for the first time. On the other hand, a babysitter with children of her own can empathize with you more easily.

Rapid Turnover

Nannies tend to move on to new jobs. Not all of them do, and not every three months. But they do tend to move after a year or 18 months. This may be due to their relative youth. They want to go on to new things or different places. It is good to talk about this before you employ someone. You could make it clear that you expect a minimum stay of 18 months. It may not be something you can enforce. But it will give your nanny a chance to decide if that is what she wants. Hopefully she will try to meet your needs as well as her own.

The trouble with fast turnover is that your child may have formed a bond. Then you have to start all over again.

What Happens While You're Out?

Some parents just don't like someone in their house when they are not there. The house may be tidy at the end of the day when you come home. But you have no way of knowing what has gone on during the day. You could stop in without notice, but that would show a lack of trust. And trust is the key to all types of childcare. Of course, to some extent trust is earned. Trust is even more critical when you have a relative stranger in your home.

Bigger Bills

With a nanny and your child at home all day you will have bigger household bills. The heat will need to be on during colder weather. And the lights and phone will also get more use.

Is the House Big Enough?

A nanny is not an option if you don't have a spare room. A nanny's room has to be bigger than a closet. A good-sized room will allow your nanny to make it cozy and a nice place to be when she is off-duty. In addition, she may not want to stay cooped up in one room when she isn't working. You need to think about the rest of your house. Is there enough room for all of you?

A Stranger in the Home

Before she has settled in, it may seem that your new nanny is a stranger to you. You will have to accept some things on faith. Nannies are not licensed. In California you can get a free background check done by calling Trustline (see Resources). And in the United States you should be able to learn whether she has ever been arrested or convicted of a sexual or child-abuse offense. Contact your local police department or Social Services office to learn how. Or, you can hire a nanny who has been trained in a professional nanny school (see Resources). These women receive thorough training and their backgrounds are checked. Ask the nanny school about their checking procedures.

Hopefully you will feel that you have checked her out well enough. But there can occasionally be a time during which you aren't quite sure. It's just getting used to having someone else around. You may wonder whether they are the nosy type, or clumsy, or won't bother to clean the bath tub.

Being Flexible

You may find some nannies are less than flexible when it comes to the rest of the house. They are not there to clean. But there is a difference between expecting them to do the cleaning and knowing that they won't mind washing and putting away a few coffee cups.

Daily Nanny

A nanny who doesn't live in will be doing the same job, but she will come to your house each day to do it. She will probably live nearby. She costs a little more in terms of salary. But she may turn out to be cheaper overall. A live-in nanny's use of the phone and food can add up.

Cathy has had the same nanny for all three of her children. But she has never lived in. *"Maria was our next-door neighbor in our last house. She had worked as a nanny when she was younger. At first, the children went to her. But when number three came along, Maria wanted to look after them in our home. I think that was because she could leave them and the mess here at the end of the day. Now we've moved. So Maria comes over here when I need her.*

"I pay her hourly, rather than by the week, because she is part-time. For three children, she is paid $12.00 an hour. When the eldest starts school, I expect I will drop her hourly rate because she'll only have two again. It works out cheaper for me to have her than to send them all to nursery school, which costs about $100.00 a week per child.

"I have complete trust in Maria. We are similar kinds of people. We're both tidy, so she leaves the house as we would both want to find it. We get along well, just as she does with the children. They love her and she loves them.

"She doesn't have to help around the house. But I often find that she's put the wash in the dryer when I come home.

"In spite of all that, though, I still do a lot for the children. That's mainly because Maria doesn't have a car. She can walk Rosie to school and pick her up. But if Rosie were sick and needed to be picked up quickly, I would do it."

The Nanny from Hell

Someone always knows someone else who has had a nanny from hell. But they are few and far between.

Sarah was looking for a nanny for her little girl when she was going back to work part time: *"This girl came from an agency. They should have checked her out. I was going back to work four days a week. The nanny came in before I started, and there was no problem at all. I was at home, and I could even hear her on the baby listener at times. I had no reason to think there would be a problem.*

"When I went back to work, though, things changed. I would get home and the place was a real mess. She'd had her friends over for lunch, which I didn't mind. But she was using our food. She used our best china, too, which she put in the dishwasher.

"If that was all, I could have overlooked it. But she'd only just started with us. And she was doing it all the time.

"One day, Emily had a cold. I decided to work from home that day. The nanny completely lost her temper. She said that she had already made plans and I was taking over. She was really angry with me. And we had a huge fight. That was the end of that nanny.

"It made me feel very guilty that I had left Emily with her. But she seemed very happy to be with her. I had no reason to think otherwise. I also learned from my friends, later, that she didn't seem like a good caregiver at the children's play group. But no one told me. I was really upset about that. I wish they'd told me.

"It's awkward now because she lives close by and I see her around. The whole thing was really awful."

Sarah suggests that parents *"follow your instincts. We felt we had done as much as we could. We had seen her often before she began. I had been at home when she first started. Jack and I felt something wasn't right. It wasn't a strong feeling, but it was there. On the other hand, Emily seemed happy. That was what mattered most to us. So what if we didn't like her? But looking back, Emily was only two and a half. She wasn't really old enough to know what the nanny was doing was wrong. Maybe Emily enjoyed all her friends, who knows?"*

To protect yourself, try some of these methods:
- Ask your friends to drop in and check on a new nanny
- Ask the nanny to go to the same toddler groups as your friends
- Follow up on references yourself, even if you use an agency
- Draw up a contract between you
- Discuss the limits of behavior you will accept. Include them in the contract.

But all nannies aren't like Sarah's.

Amy has four children and has had three nannies. They have lived both in and out. *"Our first live-in nanny came to us when my second child was 14 weeks old. She came for seven months. Then she got homesick and went back west, to her home.*

"Our second came from New Zealand. We didn't meet her until she arrived in the country. It was a little risky, but she was referred to us by a friend. And we were getting desperate. We felt it was fate that someone asked us if we needed help at that point. But on top of that, we felt we had little choice.

"She stayed with us 18 months. It was a very stable time. She wanted to move on after that. It wasn't because she didn't like it. It was just time for her to move on. You have to accept that with many nannies. Both sides were happy when she left.

"When I look back, I think we tried too hard with the first nanny. Now we feel they either will like you or they won't. They have to fit in with your family.

"Now we have a daily nanny. She's the youngest of them all. She is well trained, and she is by far the best. She has a way with children. We heard about her because she is the daughter of a friend."

Amy thinks childcare plans should vary with the size and age of your family. While a nursery school can be good for one phase, it isn't always right for every phase. And of course, children vary in what works best with *them*. She doesn't like her children to be cared for out of the house until they are more than two years old. *"The best place to have them cared for is at home. Even if you're not there, they don't have to cope with too much change. They can feel secure in the same place all the time."*

Now that her children are older (they're still all under five), she feels she's past the need for live-in care. *"But I didn't have any problems with live-in nannies. We were worried at first about her sitting in between us on the sofa. But she would go off and do her own thing at night.*

"If you want privacy, think about the sort of room she is living in. Is there a television? We also put a phone in her room.

"The only way I can get out in the morning is for the nanny to come in promptly at eight o'clock. I leave at 9:15 am, so there is an overlap. That's when I can get myself ready. We all know what we are aiming for."

Nanny Share

If you can't afford a nanny, or if you are only going back to work part-time, a nanny share may be the answer for you. Diane used a nanny-share plan: *"My son Joey was about 10 months old. I wanted to work part-time. I wanted him to be cared for at home, but I couldn't afford a full-time nanny. He had been going to a sitter, but it was such a hassle. I'm not too organized, and my work hours can vary. I really needed a nanny who was flexible. So, first of all, I placed an ad in the local paper for someone I could share a nanny with. I found a doctor who was pregnant and wanted to work for half the week. Then we found the nanny.*

"We both had two and a half days each. Our change-over day was Thursday. We also had the option of doubling up if something else came up on another day. But neither of us wanted the nanny to have both children all the time.

"Joey adjusted to the plan very well. I would work upstairs. He hardly noticed whether I was there or not. He had his own toys and his own home. It was harder as he got older. When he was about three, he got confused about which day was a mommy day and which was a nanny day. I think that was partly because my days were spread out. I think it is better to have your time in a block, so there is less confusion.

"The down side of having a Monday as one of your days is that you miss out on Monday holidays. I was doing a job where if I wasn't working, I wasn't earning. So paying for those days made a difference to me. We solved it by doubling up on the Tuesday after a Monday holiday.

"It wasn't hard for me to work from home. I knew the minute Sally came through the door, I was paying her. That was a pretty good incentive to get to work. What was hard was missing out on doing some things with Joey. For example, his music group was on a Monday. It was always Sally who took him there.

"Joey and Sally didn't disturb me when I was working. But other people don't understand a freelancer is working as much as anyone in an office. People would drop in for coffee. I solved that because I got Sally to answer the door when I was working. She would let people know I was busy and couldn't visit.

"This plan worked very well for us. Sally stayed with us for seven years. The doctor and I both went on to have second children whom she looked after too. The two sets of children became great friends. One thing I think made it work so well was that on Thursdays (changeover day) we all had lunch together: Sally, the moms and the kids. This meant we kept in touch. Sally wasn't asked to carry messages between the two of us. I think that helped us with Sally.

"Looking back, I don't think we looked at the issues of illness and vacations closely enough. We had a contract that all of us signed. We (the mothers) wanted six weeks' vacation, so we gave Sally six weeks, too. But we didn't say she had to make her vacations match ours. So one year, she had 12 weeks off! The next year we changed the contract so that she had to take four of the six weeks when we took ours.

"We also went through a stage where Sally was sick a lot. I think we should have put into the contract that she would have just so many sick days. After that she would only receive minimum sick pay. Once we had started to pay her under one set of conditions, it was very hard to change. But with a clause in your contract, there is less fuss about it.

"The plan worked well for us. The lunches helped keep it running smoothly. You do have to keep working at it and adapting it. But Sally was an important part of our life. The plan only stopped because I wanted to work longer hours, and Sally got married and wanted to start a family. But we're still in touch."

Finding a Nanny

There are a number of ways to go. They are:
- Word of mouth, contacts, friends
- Nanny and au pair agencies
- Nanny schools (see Resources)
- National Association of Child Care Resource and Referral Agencies (see Resources)
- Advertise in local paper or in any classifieds-type paper

If you go through an agency, they can do the first selection work for you. They can identify those they have registered who meet your needs. They would be able to give you a short list of suitable candidates from this group.

NANNY APPLICATION QUESTIONS

Full name _____ Telephone number _____

Full address _____

_____

Smoker? Yes / No

Total years working with children: _____

Earliest start date: _____

Previous experience:

1. Number of children _____ 2. Number of children _____ 3. Number of children _____

   Length of job _____   Length of job _____   Length of job _____

Other details _____

_____

Education and training _____

Own car? Yes / No   Have driver's license? Yes / No

Can drive? Yes / No

If no, how would get to work? _____

References

1. Personal ref _____

2. Professional refs (to be brought to interview)_____

Can I contact refs by phone? _____

Current income _____

Pay _____ Other benefits _____ Hours _____

Current duties _____

Want to interview? Yes / No

If yes, date _____   Time _____

If you don't want to use an agency, your ad may bring you a response of more- and less-suitable applicants. You will need to narrow these down to a smaller number to interview.

Telephone Interviews

You may first want to speak over the phone to applicants who respond to your ad. Interview them help you get more details and find out who are the strongest candidates. Think about your *key needs*. Work out a few questions in advance that will prompt useful answers.

Make sure that you tell the applicant when you will contact her again. If she's not on the short list, let her know that as soon as you can by phone or by mail. If you're not sure about her, say so. It's better to be direct and open. Don't fudge the issue so the candidate is misled.

Face-to-Face Interviews

Think about where you will interview. You both need to feel at ease. What about your child, or children? You will want them to meet the nanny, but you may not want them to interrupt the interview. It may be worth having another person there who can take them into the yard or another part of the home when you want to focus on the nanny. If you have a partner, it could be helpful for both of you if he is there. It helps when you talk things over later on.

Plan the Interview

You need to have more than a chat. Write down what the job entails. Give the candidate a copy.

Make sure you have read their resume *before* the interview. Nothing is worse for a candidate than to be asked questions that make it clear you haven't read it well. Remember, she is judging you, too, and making a decision about whether she wants to work with you.

Make a list of the questions that you want answered. Think about how they relate to the job.

INTERVIEW QUESTIONS

Name:

Training:

Any formal training?

Are the certificates available? Yes/No

Any other qualifications?

Where was the training?

What was the training like?

Why are you a nanny?

Experience:

How many previous jobs?

How many children (including age and sex)?

How long did each job last?

What were the reasons for leaving each job?

To what extent was the applicant left in complete charge of the children in each job situation?

References:

Available? Yes/No

Can I contact them directly?

Home and background:

Where do you live?

What do your parents do?

How do you get along with your parents?

Any other close family?

Do you have any children?

Do you get homesick?

Other details:

Do you smoke? Yes/No

Do you drive? Yes/No

Any driving offenses?

Do you own a car?

Religious?

What hobbies do you have?

Local knowledge:

Do you know the area?

Do you have family and friends nearby?

Health:

Overall level of health

Any recurring illnesses?

Major operations?

Children:

What do you prefer in terms of age/sex?

How would you entertain the children?

What are your views on discipline?

Personal responsibility for children:

What are your feelings about being left in charge of the children?

How do you feel about responsibility?

What about dangers in the house (ask questions about common emergencies)?

The future:

What are your ambitions?

Where do you see yourself in two to five years?

How long do you see yourself staying with us?

Put the Candidate at Ease

Think of an ice breaker. Maybe you can find something on her resume to start the interview with. Or, ask why she chose to work with children.

Make sure you won't be interrupted. Organize the children's activity in advance. Make sure the phone is off the hook or the answering machine is on. If you have friends who tend to drop by, warn them that this is Interview Day.

Be open, fair and honest. The interview is a two-way process. Your candidates are there to find out about you, as well as the job. Don't assume that they will want the job.

Listen

It is a common mistake in an interview to spend too much time talking. It's easy to talk for ages about your children, particularly with a potential nanny. But that's not the purpose of the interview.

Spend 80% of the time listening and 20% talking.

Ask Open Questions

An open question elicits a more detailed response than a yes-or-no question. You could ask, "Do you enjoy playing with babies?" Or you could say, "What do you like about spending time with a baby?"

The second question will prompt a fuller response than the first. You will get more clues about a person by trying asking as many open questions as possible and letting her talk.

Another example would be, "My child is a fussy eater. Will you be able to deal with that?" It may be better to ask, "Tell me about working with different children when it hasn't been very easy."

Beware of Prejudging

You could lose out on the best candidate if you reject her because you react to her appearance. I know a nanny who is covered with tattoos. She might cause a lot of people to gasp when she first appears. But she is excellent at her job. It would be easy to prejudge her. But an employer would be missing out on a capable, caring nanny.

Ending the Interview

Agree on what will happen next. Say how many people you will interview. If you can't contact them for a week, say so. Try to learn what the candidate's level of interest is. It may be useful to you when you decide.

Don't Forget to Take References

Check that the references are recent. If not, why not? Be sure you can call people to talk to them about her. This is vital. You need to feel secure in your choice. Talking to others who have worked with her will help you make a decision.

Plan to Take about an Hour

By the time you have explained the duties involved, you won't have much time for asking questions. Keep them brief.

Some people find it useful to take an instant photo of the candidates. If you do so, make sure that the candidate is happy with this.

It's probably best not to schedule more than three interviews in a day.

On page 120 is Alex's sample interview sheet. It's useful for reviewing the types of questions you might want to ask.

This is only one person's list of questions. The questions on it may differ from the ones that matter to you. But it may give you some good ideas. It helps to prepare something like it in advance of the interview. It gives you something to work from. It may help you remember to ask something vital. Note-taking is also useful. Your candidate may want to take notes too.

Contracts

Once you have chosen a nanny, clearly define duties, salary, vacations and so on. Write everything down in one document, agreed to by all parties. The contract is a good way to resolve disputes at a later date. You can make up your own contract. Both parties sign it to say that they agree with everything in it. A contract can be enforced by law as long as it doesn't violate any laws. That would make it void.

You can make a verbal contract, which might be legal. But it would be much more difficult to prove than a written contract. It helps to have a document to refer to. Then all parties know what is expected of them.

On the next page is a sample contract one mother used with her nanny. The contract clearly lays out the nature of the employment. Not every contract has to be as detailed as this one. But it may be helpful to both employer and nanny. Other caregivers, such as au pairs and mother's helpers, are self-employed. Therefore, although you may prefer some sort of contract, it does not have to be so detailed.

A final word from a mother who chose her nanny from an interview: *"First of all, I got along with her. She brought her resume along, which appealed to my sense of order. She had worked as a volunteer with children. This showed me that she liked being with them. She had a good education, which mattered to me. When I asked her what she might do with the children during the day, her thoughts were like mine. The questions she asked were revealing too. She wanted to know my views on discipline. She wanted to know what would happen if we disagreed on an issue like that. It seemed to me she was committed. And I was right. We are very happy with her."*

SAMPLE OF AN EMPLOYMENT CONTRACT

Employer's name _____

Employee's name _____

Social Security\Social Insurance # _____ Employment will begin on ____

Job title: Nanny

Basic hours:

Monday - Friday, 7:45 am to 6 pm

Extra hours:

One evening per week babysitting is required. Time off will be given in lieu of babysitting (normally Wednesday morning till 11 am).

Any extra babysitting will be paid at a rate of _____ per hour.

Duties

- Provide supervised daily care for children
- Plan, purchase foods for, prepare and serve three daily meals (one hot) to children
- Help the children develop their minds and bodies
- Arrange for and take children to doctors or dentists, as needed. Always advise mother first, except in an emergency. In an emergency, take care of the child's needs first, then contact either parent as soon as you can.
- Keep children's rooms tidy
- Plan daily and weekly schedules to include both indoor and outdoor activities, play groups and lessons
- Wash and dry children's clothes
- Wash and dry children's bedding weekly
- Shop for all children's clothes and other child or baby items (such as diapers)
- Make sure no one smokes in the house
- Make sure no animals are brought into the house
- Straighten up toys and after meals each day

Salary

$_____ per week, paid weekly after the first week. Standard tax deductions will be taken and payments made on behalf of employee.

A salary review will take place once each year.

Vacation Days: Three weeks per year, plus all federal holidays. You may choose two weeks' vacation each year, for which notice is required. This should be taken at a convenient time for both parties. Remaining vacation days should be taken at the same time as your employer's.

Employee Signature: _____ Date: _____

Employer Signature: _____ Date: _____

EMPLOYMENT CONTRACT, CONTINUED

Car

You will have use of a car and gas when on duty. Please let us know when the car needs more gas. If you use your own car to carry out duties, you will receive a mileage allowance of _____ per mile.

Telephone

Itemized calls that do not exceed $_____ per month are allowed.

Refreshments

Refreshments for yourself while on duty are included. So are refreshments for other nannies and the children in their care.

Sick Pay

You will receive up to two weeks of paid sick leave per year. Notify employer as soon as possible of any illness that prevents you from working. Such notice should be given no later than 7:00 am on the day in question so other plans can be made.

Pension

We do not offer a pension plan.

Confidentiality

It is a condition of employment that now and at all times in the future the employee shall keep the affairs and concerns of the household, and its business, confidential. The only exception is that which may be required by law.

Discipline

Reasons that may give cause for discipline include:

1. Job incompetence

2. Not reliable with regard to time

3. Failure to comply with instructions

4. Conduct during or after hours prejudicial to the family

If required, discipline will proceed as follows:

1. First verbal warning

2. Second verbal warning

3. Dismissal with four weeks' notice

The following actions would lead to immediate dismissal:

1. Theft

2. Substance abuse, including drunkenness

3. Child abuse

4. Acting in an unsafe manner with children

Termination

In the first four weeks of employment, one week's notice is required by either party. After four weeks' work, either party may terminate the employment by giving two weeks' notice.

Initial (employee): _____

Initial (employer): _____

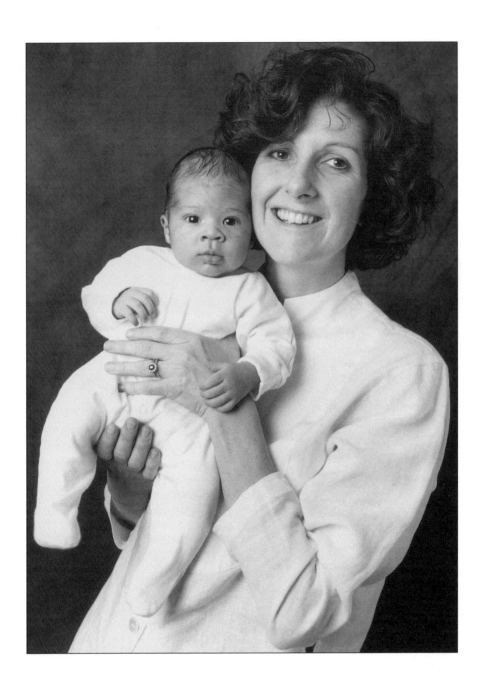

Chapter 9

Au Pairs and Other Support

Nannies tend to fill a long-term need. They often have experience and a desire to blend in with the family. Other caregivers who look after your child at your home, such as doulas or mother's helpers, may only do so for a short time. Or they may take on the job as a path to another goal. Au pairs, for example, often want to learn English or improve their fluency.

Postpartum Doulas

"Doula" is an ancient Greek word. Today it refers to a woman who has experience in childbirth. A doula provides physical and emotional support to a mother before, during and after childbirth. She also provides information.

A postpartum doula will come to live in your home after you have given birth. She can help with the baby, the housework and with older children. She can help you solve breastfeeding problems. She is there to provide information and support to a new mother.

A postpartum doula's training is focused. A doula helps smooth the transition after childbirth for the mother. When your life as a new mother has settled down and is more or less under control again, her work is done.

The cost of a postpartum doula varies, but they aren't cheap. Still, the focused, caring service they provide can make a huge difference. If you think you'd like to employ a postpartum doula, plan well in advance.

Postpartum doulas are not widely available. Plan to interview and select your postpartum doula a few months before you are due to give birth. Contact Doulas of North America (DONA) for referral to doulas near you (see Resources).

Mother's Helpers

If you need ongoing help around the house as well as with children, you may try a mother's helper.

A mother's helper may not have formal training. She works a full day and often lives with the family. If she comes from a foreign country, she might want to study English at night. You can tell her just what you want her to do to help around the house. But the word "help" is the key. They are there to *help* you, not to *replace* you. Occasionally, of course, you might leave the children in their care. But it isn't likely this kind of support would suit a mother with more than a part-time job.

Au Pair

"Au pair" means "on a par with." This means an au pair should be treated like a member of the family. An au pair is most likely a young woman from western Europe between 18 and 25 years of age. She lives in the home for a year and performs childcare, but no heavy housework. She can work up to 5 hours a day. She should have two days off each week. Her purpose for being in the country is to learn the language and culture. She should have a chance to attend school.

Au pairs receive:
- A private room
- Air fare
- $100.00 a week
- Medical insurance
- Up to $500.00 toward education

Eight au pair agencies have met federal guidelines. For a fee they screen applicants and match them with families. But try to choose your au pair yourself, from a group the agency provides. Find out about their childcare experience and why they want to come to North America. Make sure the agency will replace your au pair if she doesn't work out. The United States Information Agency (U.S.I.A.) will provide you with a list of the approved agencies (see Resources).

As of 1995, an au pair who comes to the United States through a federally approved agency is subject to new guidelines. She must complete up to 32 hours of training in health, safety and child development. And to work in a family with a child under two years of age, she must be able to document at least six months of infant or childcare experience.

Benefits of the Au Pair System

Cost Effective

If you have space in your house, then an au pair is a cheap way to combine childcare and household help.

Serves Both Your Needs

Your au pair is here to learn English, so she will want to be involved with you and your family. She will be paid for what she does, which gives her pocket money, too.

Babysitting Service

You can be flexible with the hours your au pair works. She may be willing to trade a long day's work for a long weekend off to do some traveling, for example. There is no rule that says her hours have to be done during the day. So you could get babysitting done by her, too. If you want more sitting, you could pay her extra for it.

Another Culture

The good news is an au pair can teach your children about another culture. Just as the au pair is learning something new, so are your children. Your children will learn about a different country and the way things are done there. They may also pick up some of the language. But the bad news is . . . the au pair may know few English words, at first. This may make it harder for the children to speak with her.

Problems with Au Pairs

She May Not Like Children

It is possible. She is in the country to learn about our culture. She may go through the motions of caring for children. And she may do so very well. But she doesn't have to want to be with them all the time.

More on Your Plate

Someone said that having an au pair is a little like looking after your friend's teenage daughter. She will be more one more person for you to look after. She may be only 17. She may need some guidance about "life" in general. It really depends on the au pair you select.

No Contract

The agreement is not bound by a contract. If she wants to go somewhere else, she will go. But you may have a contract with the agency that helped you obtain your au pair. If you paid a fee for this service, and things don't work out with your au pair, the agency should help you find another au pair.

Car Insurance

You will need to extend your car insurance if she is to have use of the car. This could be costly if she is a young driver.

Heather runs an au pair-and-nanny agency. *"If only I had a farm to grow au pairs. They are very much in demand. An au pair is likely to want a nice family atmosphere and not too much work. Make sure they know your rules. Don't expect too much of them. Remember they are young girls! They need to be told what they can and can't do. They tend to stay for six months to a year."*

Louisa has used both nannies and au pairs, so she can compare them. *"I think there are times in your life when one makes more sense than the other. After my first child was born, I used a nursery school. But when I had my second, I started to use a nanny. I worked three days a week at that point. Having someone in the house was the simplest method of childcare for me. It was also cheaper with two children. When our third child, Scott, was born, I was back at work again within three or four weeks. I must have been crazy, but they needed me at work.*

"But Scott was diagnosed with leukemia when he was six months old. We spent from May to November in a hospital. Our nanny was coming in three days a week. She offered to come in for an extra day for free, which was really good of her. But we felt we had to pay her. Having a nanny at this stage was great. We couldn't have used an au pair. We needed someone to work longer hours than that, and who had a commitment to childcare. The older two children were having to take a back seat to Scott's illness.

"Once the greatest danger was over and Scott was home, I really had to be with him. Now I wasn't working at all. We couldn't really afford a nanny four days a week. We were sorry to have to let her go. I started thinking about getting an au pair—mainly as another pair of hands.

"We had grown so used to our nanny. It was hard to start over again with a stranger, building up trust and so on. I was concerned at first about behavior problems. But there really haven't been any. You have to be broad-minded, and give some leeway. But you can spot abuse of the phone, and things like that, with itemized phone bills, for example."

Other parents who have hired au pairs share what it was like:

"What I like about the au pairs we've had is that they are flexible. They've been great with school-age children. They can babysit for a couple of evenings a week too."

"You tend to get problems of adolescence: romance, late nights, losing privacy."

"If they like children, it's a plus. But not all of them do. Try to find out if they have brothers or sisters."

"It's good to have an extra pair of hands. I just wanted someone for two or three hours here and there. I didn't want someone around the whole day."

"We are lucky to have enough space. But you have to make the girl feel as though it's her home and she's part of the family. You may have to compromise on your privacy. But it can be worth it."

"Don't expect too much from them."

"It gives you time to do things the children don't want to do, and time to go off on your own."

Finding an Au Pair

Again, like nannies, a lot of agencies, both in this country and in others, can supply au pairs. But only a few agencies have federal approval.

An agency may charge a sign-up fee (but not all do). A placement fee may be charged in addition, when the right person has been found for you. Sometimes a trial period of two to four weeks is involved.

Jenny runs a nanny-and-au pair agency. She has this advice to offer about au pairs: *"They are in demand, so it's worth taking care of them. If you expect them to do too much work or babysitting, don't be surprised if they leave for a better job elsewhere. Having an au pair is great if you've got the right one."*

ISSUES PARENTS NEED TO DISCUSS

Trust

Trust is key. If you are not happy with some aspect of your au pair's behavior, discuss it openly with her. You may have misunderstood her.

Privacy

Try to make her privacy as important as yours. Make her own room as nice as you can. Be prepared to give up some of your privacy for the time your au pair is with you.

Emergencies

Ask your au pair if she has a basic knowledge of first aid. If not, why not go to a one-day course with her? (Contact your local chapter of the Red Cross.)

Sex, Smoking and Other Vices

There's no reason why your caregiver shouldn't be sexually active. But what about in your house? If you don't mind, say so. And if you do, say so too. Honesty will prevent awkward moments later on. The same would apply to anything else that you don't want to happen in your house.

Use and Abuse of Your Home

Where do you draw the line between taking advantage of your home and feeling like part of the family? It varies from person to person. It is worth thinking about what is and isn't all right with you. Be clear and direct from the start. Then there is no chance you will be misunderstood.

Chapter 10

Informal Childcare and After-School Options

Changing Needs

Your needs change as your children and family grow. There is a time in your family's life when childcare must come first. When your child is very young, the caregiver has to be gentle but firm. With toddlers, the caregiver should watch closely so that as your children discover the world, they aren't harmed by it. Toddlers need someone to speak with who can explain the world to them. They need someone to guide them as they develop. And they need someone to give them a safe haven from which to reach out as they start to socialize.

From nursery school through their later school years, your children will be left with other watchful adults. But they still need to be accompanied here and there. And if they are not to be "latchkey kids," they must be supervised after school.

Then there is the "awkward" stage, when your children are not quite adults, although they are quite capable of being on their own much of the time. At this stage, they need support, but they don't need looking after. (They could be about 14 or 15.) What do you do with them then?

> ### QUESTIONS TO ASK YOURSELF ABOUT YOUR CHILDREN
>
> Are they mature? Are they responsible? Do they have a good sense of safety precautions?
>
> Do they feel happy about being left by themselves? Are they nervous about it?
>
> Where do you live? Is it close to school? Can they ride home with someone? Is there someone they can call on if they want to?
>
> How long will they be alone? Can you plan things so they aren't left alone every night?

You may feel that, however old your child is, they still need formal childcare. You might prefer them to go to a caregiver after school. Another option is informal childcare through a neighbor, a friend or a relative. This person may also have children but doesn't work, or works different hours. It is worth exploring all options. These plans can be flexible and cheap. And you can count on them. Often no money changes hands. You just return the favor.

Neighbors

Sally chose to use a network of neighbors. *"I live in a small housing tract. There are neighbors who stay at home. They know the children are around and can check on them. It may not be ideal but it's only for an hour or so."*

Neighbors can be a great source of support. How well do you know yours? Many parents find that spending time at home after their baby is born is the first time they become acquainted with their neighbors. Parent support groups or religious groups are also useful. They can help introduce people to one another. Sometimes it is hard to make that first move and talk to someone you don't know. But it can often pay off in terms of new friends with lives like your own.

Laura's little girl has now started school. But she goes home with her neighbor's children. She's there for just over an hour before Laura comes home from work. *"I pay my neighbor for doing this for me. She has a nanny who picks up the kids, but I have to do my share. The point is, if you can't return the favor, then you should pay up."*

Friends and Neighbors

Not only neighbors can help with childcare. You can make plans with others you have gotten to know through toddler groups, postnatal groups and so on.

Carolyn was going back to work sooner than she had planned. She felt this event was a big enough disruption to her family. She didn't want to introduce them to a stranger in addition. *"My husband's job was flexible. At first we could juggle pick-ups. My son, Tom, was going through a transition time. He was just starting at playgroup and I didn't want him* to have to cope with other changes. So Mike managed to pick him up. Minnie, who had started nursery school, was picked up by Anna, whom she already knew from the playgroup.*

"Although Anna wasn't trained in childcare, I felt safer letting Minnie go with someone I knew. I worried about leaving my kids with someone I hadn't known very long. It also meant it was less for the children to get used to.

YOU ARE RESPONSIBLE

Remember that it is the parents who are responsible for their children until they are 18. Although others may care for them, it is parents, in the end, who must ensure their well-being.

"In fact, Tom has settled in very well at playgroup. So on the days I work, Anna takes him home with her and then picks up Minnie after school. It helps that she's got plenty of videos for Tom to watch. We don't have a television at home, and Tom loves them."

Angela solved her own childcare problems by sharing childcare with a friend who was also an airline stewardess. *"When I had my first baby, I didn't plan to go back to work. My options were full-time or nothing. I took my maternity leave of seven months and kept my options open. I'm glad I did because things started to change. More choices opened up for the cabin crew.*

"I went for an option that meant I worked no more than half a working month. The nature of the job meant I would need childcare at different times. My family all live out of state, so they couldn't help. But I had a friend who was in the same business. She didn't have any family support either. We decided to take each other's children for two weeks each.

"One good thing about this system was that our children grew up like brother and sister. They got very close. They each gained a playmate and learned how to socialize. And they were still with people they knew.

"Another plus was that it cost nothing. And that has to be a major factor when it comes to childcare.

"But there were things that weren't so good. We both felt we didn't have enough time of our own with our children. We were either working for two weeks, or we were caring for the two of them. There was nothing in between. Besides, it could only work when we had a total of two children. Now I've had another little one. And my friend is pregnant. Neither of us

could cope with four children, even if we wanted to. Think about going shopping with four! On second thought, don't! You wouldn't be able to take them anywhere. So although it was good for a while, and saw us both through that early stage, it couldn't last forever."

Relatives

This can be a rich source of support. The day-to-day support that families used to be able to give is now less practical as we become a more mobile society. But there are many benefits to keeping childcare within the family:

- Cost
  Childcare is expensive. Many people simply can't afford caregivers, nannies or preschools. If you are lucky enough to have access to good, free childcare, use it!

- A pleasure, not a burden
  Many grandparents are pleased to be more involved with their growing family. Childcare may be a special pleasure if they have retired or one of them is left on his or her own. They may be pleased to be asked. And they know they are helping out. However, they are not as young as they used to be, and small children can be tiring. Don't allow a pleasure to become a burden.

- People your children know
  There are no new faces or people to get used to. These are people whom the children have known all their lives. They are almost as familiar as you are, if they live close by.

- Children are in touch with "older people"
  It seems a shame that we tend to mix with our own age group and no other. It starts with preschool groups, and seems to go on from there. Teens mix with teens. Young single people mix with other young, single people. And older people mix with other older people. There's a lot to be said for having friends in the same peer group. But we can often gain a great deal from mixing friendships across age groups. The benefits to both child and grandparent are clear. Both can learn and gain from the other.

- Can still leave them if sick
  If your child were very ill, you might want to look after them yourself. But in most cases, your relatives are glad to help out. By contrast, a sitter or a preschool may ask you to keep your child at home until they feel better.

- They know what your standards are
  The nice thing about leaving your children with family members is that so much is already known. Your family will know what you expect. They know how you behave toward the children. They know what the children should be doing. If the children aren't allowed candy during the day, your relative already knows that. But sometimes life isn't so simple. They may know how you do it, but decide to do it their way. That could cause a rift. Or you may try to ignore it because they provide so much help and you don't want to upset your family.

Lydia is now back at work. Her son Jeremy is being cared for by her mother, who lives close by. *"My mother offered to look after Jeremy when I went back to work. She cares for her other grandson, Will, too. She has a disability, but she said the babysitting would keep her going. Her help made it so much simpler for me. I found it hard to go back to work anyway. This really eased the process. It helped that he'd spent time at his grandma's and knew her so well. He and Will get on really well, too. Will is more outgoing. But Jeremy has learned to hold his own.*

"It's so good to have family close by. But naturally there is also a down side. For example, if you pay someone, you can say what you want. It's harder for me to do that. Mom won't take any money. But she's bought a double stroller, highchairs, diapers—you name it. My indebtedness makes it tough to be critical. It sounds ungrateful, which I'm not. I have to be sensitive about some things. Jeremy has a coat I really like, but Mom can't stand it. She always puts him in something else. That makes me more determined that he wear it.

"But, I think she's sensitive, too. She knows when to back off. And she keeps quiet at the right moment.

"We have always been supportive of each other as a family. Now we all babysit for each other. We have Sunday lunch as a family. It's noisy because of all the children. But it's also a lot of fun."

Are There Any Problems?

Before you ask your parents to give childcare, it may be worth thinking it over very hard. Was there something about your upbringing that was tough for you in your own childhood? What if this comes up again while your parents are caring for your children? Is it easy for you to be direct with your parents? Or do they still have some control over you? How would you react if they did something you didn't like? Would you be able to talk it over? Or would you both revert to a parent/child relationship?

Even if you don't use informal childcare most of the time, it could be useful when you need childcare on short notice. What if your sitter calls to say that her daughter has chickenpox and she can't take your child for two weeks? You would need someone to fill the gap.

School Days

If your child just needs care after school, you could still ask a friend, neighbor or relative to help out. Or you could check out after-school sitters, after-school play groups and kids' clubs. There are more women working, more single-parent families and youth crime has increased. After-school and vacation-time care will continue to grown as a major issue for parents and policymakers alike.

After-School Sitters

If you are using a sitter, she may be willing to keep looking after your child as he grows, and to do things such as pick him up and drop him off at school or activities. If you want her to do this, think about where you want your child to go to school. How easy will that be for the sitter? Does she have a car? Does she have children that have to be picked up from another school at the same time?

It may be hard to find a sitter near you who prefers just to have children after school, when her own children are at home anyway. But ask around. Often such sitters are most easily found by word of mouth. Ask other parents what they do. Ask your own children what their friends do.

After-School Play

There are different types of after-school playgroups. Some are run by schools, from, say, 3:30 pm until 5:30 or 6:00 pm. Local volunteer groups may also run them, on a free-of-charge, first-come, first-served basis. Some churches and temples run programs. You may want to know if there are any nearby schools that run them before you choose which school to apply for.

John is a "play manager" for his town. *"We have six play centers. They are open-access. That means the children come and go. They don't have to be dropped off and picked up at prearranged times. The centers are open 52 weeks a year. When school is in session, they run from 5:00 pm until 9:00 pm. School-vacation hours are from 11:00 am until 8:00 pm. They are aimed at all children between the ages of five and 16.*

"We also offer an after-school club. It has a bus to pick up children from local schools and take them to one school until the parents' pick-up time. During summer vacation, they plan a lot of fun events. Some cost about $8.00 to $10.00 a day and last from 11:00 am until 3:00 pm. There is also day care, which costs more, about $75.00 to $125.00 a week, but this is from 8:30 am until 5:30 pm, for 5- to 12-year-olds."

Private After-School Programs

Private after-school programs are often run in a building attached to a primary school. When school is over, the staff meets the children who

are staying after school on the playground. They have a snack, and then play games like tag. It provides a safe place and a chance to play with friends until they are picked up by their parents.

Private Schools

Some private schools have "prep time" after school. This means children can stay and be supervised while they do their homework. This gives the parents some extra time before picking them up. And it gets the homework out of the way.

Overall, there is still a great shortage of after-school care. No state or province has enough licensed childcare slots for the children who need them.

School Vacations

So you've got your children taken care of during the school year. But then the school vacations arrive. You may have to think of some new options for these times.

Perhaps this is the time when grandparents who live far away could help. Why not send your children to stay with them for two weeks? The children would likely love it—an adventure away from home. They could feel secure with their grandparents. And of course it would give *you* a break. You would have a chance to act spontaneously again, to go out without having to find a sitter three weeks in advance, for example.

Annual Vacations

Some parents find this one of the hardest things to accept. No longer can you take your vacation during the school year, when prices are cut in half and the beaches are empty! Some parents are happy to take their children out of school for a couple of weeks. This may be cheaper and more relaxing. But it doesn't help solve the search for childcare during school vacations.

School Friends

As children grow up, they make new school friends. Maybe you can plan to have parents take turns caring for a small group of friends for a day or two.

Local Programs

Again, local groups, churches and temples may run programs throughout the summer. They may be run privately. Many don't cost much. Children seem to enjoy them. Some don't start till 9:30 or 10:00 am, and finish at 3:30 pm. You might alternate weeks and share the burden of being the "taxi service" to and from the activity with your partner or a friend.

Private Programs

More and more companies are seeing an obvious need for employees' children to be cared for safely while their parents are working. School vacations often present such a problem.

Janie works for a company that will be running a summer camp. *"This is the third year we've had the camp. We expanded to 75 children last year. This year there is room for 100, because it is so popular. Because this is a big company, we have the space and the demand to run our own camp. But I know smaller companies often pool together and do the same for their employees.*

"This camp is offered to the children of all employees, male or female, full- or part-time. The children range from 5-year-olds up to about 13 or 14.

For parents, what this does is take away the worry of childcare for a few weeks. It is paid for, in part, by the company. And children can sign up for one week or six weeks, or the same days (such as Wednesdays) over that period. We offer a range of things to do. We have a couple of outings each week.

"As employers look for workers, they need to be able to offer something to working parents. I think this is a good thing to offer as part of an employment package."

David runs a play program: *"We sometimes get a contract to work with one company. Or we rent a school or another safe building, and smaller companies can buy a certain number of places to be filled by their employees' children.*

"There's no fixed time for the children to arrive. They can get there any time between 8:00 am and 10:00 am. That time is for free play. The children choose what they want to do. There's a video corner, dressing-up, computers, table tennis, ball games and team games. During the day they can try archery, aerobics, badminton, basketball, face painting, video filming.

"We have between 24 and 100 children, depending on the camp. They stay in the same group all week. Each week follows a different theme. Our ratio of caregivers to children is 1:8 maximum.

"We try to make sure that each child gets a chance to do the things he or she wants to do. Our staff is most often people who have taken child-related courses and have worked with children before. This isn't just a summer job."

Programs like these are on the increase. In addition, both day and live-in summer camps are established around the country.

None of these options are cheap. But they do give your children a lot to do in an active but safe place. If you consider a summer camp for your child, find out if the program is licensed. Ask how the staff is trained and about safety. Check out the program with your local Social Services department.

If you think your colleagues could benefit from such a program, why not suggest it to your manager. She or he may realize it would benefit the company as much as the company's employees.

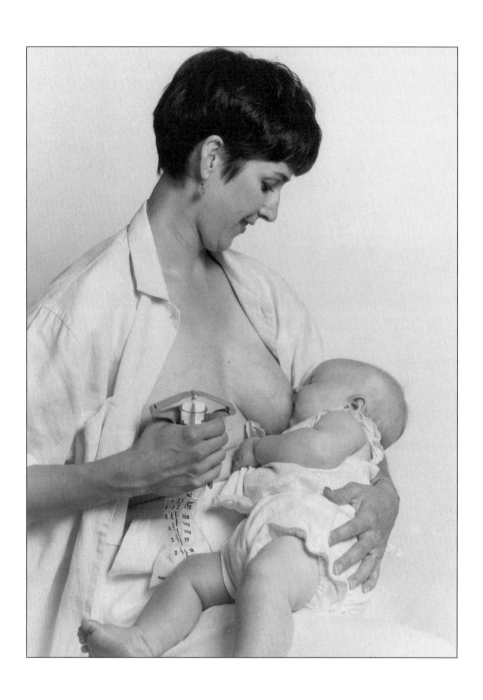

Chapter 11

Breastfeeding and Work

One of the issues of going back to work is when or whether to wean your baby from the breast. Some people will have stopped breastfeeding by this point. But if you haven't, this chapter is for you.

The best decision will be based on your own life. What do you prefer? What upsets your family least? There are no right or wrong answers, just what is right or wrong for you. It's not easy to go from 100% nurturing to spreading oneself across a number of roles. Spend some time thinking about how to make the journey as smooth as you can. It will pay off!

If you decide to keep breastfeeding when you go back to work, you may think about:

- The age of your baby

- The method of feeding till now

- The work style you will adopt

- What your baby prefers

- Your feelings

Your feelings might be the key factor to consider. Some mothers like to make a "clean break" from the role of nursing mother and primary caregiver. This isn't because they no longer want to be with their child. But some mothers find their different roles hard to combine. Such mothers prefer to settle into a new work schedule with clear boundaries. Others prefer to keep breastfeeding. These mothers find it's easier to return to work when they maintain the closeness of nursing.

Do You Have to Stop Breastfeeding?

There is no reason to stop breastfeeding when you return to work. Your body can adjust to any change in supply, with a bit of warning (more on that later). Most people who breastfeed don't find it easy all the time. And it won't be as easy as when you are at home full-time. But nursing mothers who work often feel a great sense of achievement. They feel good to be giving their baby the best source of nutrition, even when they have to be away for part of the day.

Nursing is less of a problem for those who work at home. The mother can simply breastfeed during her lunch hour, or on a break. But for those who work away from home, it can be harder. The thought of giving up nursing and being away from the baby at the same time can seem traumatic. It can also change your perspective on the whole process. For instance, some mothers simply assume that they will give up nursing when they return to work. Then they find the baby won't take a bottle. This can kindle feelings of guilt in a mother who may feel some guilt anyway: "Not only am I leaving my baby, but she will starve when I am away, too."

Having a deadline to meet can put too much pressure on a woman at this time. It is worth doing some creative thinking. Sometimes the answer is there, staring at you, but you're too upset to see it. You might ask your employer for an extra month's leave while you sort things out. They may say yes. Stranger things have happened! Or, you keep breastfeeding. This lets you maintain that special closeness with your baby. Breastfeeding can make the separation less dramatic for both of you. While one big thing has changed in your lives, another is staying just the same.

Sometimes a mother decides to give up breastfeeding as she prepares to return to work. But then she finds the whole process too difficult. She changes her mind and decides to keep nursing. The sense of relief at this point can be immense. It can also really have an effect on how the mother feels about going back to work. Breastfeeding can make the transition much more positive.

Reasons to Continue Breastfeeding

A Good, Nurturing Start

Laura found the closeness of early-morning breastfeeding a good way to start the day. *"You are on the go all day, whether you go out to work or not. So it's good to start with a relaxing cuddle in bed. The two of you can spend those extra few minutes in bed. You don't have to run downstairs to warm the bottle while the baby cries and your own eyes are barely open."* The hormone that makes milk is most active at night. That means you will have plenty of milk in the morning. So your baby gets a good, nutritious start to her day.

Maintaining the Bond

Breastfeeding is something only a baby's mother can do for her. And that can be important, especially if she is going to be left with someone else. It means that you are without doubt her mother. You provide her with something that only you, as her mother, can give.

That Relaxing Time ...

One of the great things about breastfeeding is that you have to sit down when you do it (most of the time). For the working mother, this is a benefit to take full advantage of! It is a chance to sit and relax and know that your baby is being satisfied at the same time. There are not many moments you can do this. You are likely to be praised for sitting, with your feet up, relaxing with your baby. Make the most of it!

"I had a lot of trouble starting. I'll be darned if I'm going to stop now."
—Kerry

Lots of mothers, like Kerry, find it pretty rough when they start breastfeeding. But they stick it out. It can sometimes take about six weeks for the system to settle down. If you return to work when your baby is about three months, there is barely time to enjoy it before you stop. This is why Kerry wasn't going to stop. She had worked too hard to get breastfeeding going. She says, *"I had lots of trouble for weeks after the birth. I was cracked and bleeding. But I held on because I really wanted to do it. Also, I had a Cesarean, so I really felt I wanted to do the breastfeeding right. I was depressed for the first eight weeks. I thought that was due to my problems with breastfeeding. But after that, it went like a dream."* Once you do reach the stage where you find breastfeeding a complete joy, it seems such a shame to stop.

If you are going back to work and your baby is still really young, breastfeeding helps you feel more secure. You know that the baby is still getting the best food.

Breastfeeding—How It Works

Two hormones, oxytocin and prolactin, make breastfeeding work. They produce the milk. One causes the reflex that gets the milk out of your breast and into the baby's mouth. The other maintains your supply. The baby's suckling makes your body produce more milk. It isn't just a case of the baby sucking out the milk. The baby's suckling stimulates those hormones. It gets your production process working. You and your baby work as a team to make enough milk.

Supply and Demand

The baby, when fed on demand, makes you create the right amount of milk. *Demand feeding* means giving the breast when it is asked for. Breastfeeding counselors are often asked how to estimate the amount of milk the baby is getting. You can see how much the baby is taking with a bottle, but not with a breast. But if your breasts are not sore, and your baby has wet and dirty diapers, it must be coming from somewhere! If she is gaining weight and seems happy after nursing, it's likely your baby is getting just the amount she needs. Trust yourself. You can make just the right amount, even though you can't see it.

Let-down Reflex

This is the mother's response to the baby's suckling. Some mothers find that their breasts tingle when it starts to happen. What happens is the breasts are starting to send the milk down to the areola for the baby to take. The areola is the dark part of the breast around the nipple. There is always milk there for the baby from the start of the feeding. But the let-down sends more. If you have a good supply, you may find that your other breast starts to drip when the let-down happens. And the let-down doesn't only happen when your baby is nursing. Sometimes it is triggered when you see a baby, hear a baby cry or think about your baby. But not every mother experiences it. Often, if it happens, it happens in the first weeks. It goes away once the supply is established.

The Baby's Position at the Breast

Get the baby in the right position at the breast! This is a key factor in successful breastfeeding. If the baby isn't well positioned, she may:

- Hurt you. A poorly positioned baby can make nursing quite painful. It can cause cracked or bleeding nipples. This can make breastfeeding an agony.

- Reduce your milk supply. A poorly positioned baby often sucks on the nipple instead of the areola. This means she is not sending a strong enough message to your body to make more milk.

- Want frequent feeding. There's no getting away from it: Many breastfed babies nurse more often than bottle-fed babies do. But the baby who is nursing in the wrong position may not be getting enough breast milk. That's because her mouth isn't open wide enough. She will be hungry sooner than she needs to be.

FACT FILE ON GOODNESS

Breast milk is a changing fluid. It adapts to the needs and age of the baby.

"During the first year of breastfeeding the protein content of breast milk [slowly] falls. [This happens] regardless of the mother's diet. This is . . . [because] most babies are started on solid foods from about six months . . . [These] provide the extra protein [needed] for growth. [As the protein falls, there is a normal slowing] in growth rate."

Stanway & Stanway: *Breast is Best* 1983. London, England: Pan.

Breastfeeding protects against infection.

"Breastfeeding during the first 13 weeks of life [protects] against . . . illness. [This protection] persists beyond the period of breastfeeding itself."

Howie, et al: *"Positive Effect of Breastfeeding Against Infection,"* BMJ Vol. 300, 6.1.90.

Where there is love, there is oxytocin.

"Oxytocin is involved in foreplay and in male and female orgasm. It is also released before and during suckling the baby. Oxytocin is the hormone of altruism, the forgetting of oneself." The . . . effect of this is that breastfeeding is not only good for the baby, it is good for the mother too. It helps her relax and unwind. There can be a deep sigh of relief as the milk flows to the baby. The mother can sit, relax, and enjoy. The pressures of life slip away.

Odent: *The Nature of Birth and Breastfeeding,* 1992. London, England: Bergin & Garvey.

If you are having problems with breastfeeding, contact a breastfeeding counselor or a La Leche League leader (see Resources). She can talk with you about your needs. The services of a La Leche League leader are free. You don't have to say you plan to breastfeed for any set period of time. Counselors will also support mothers who want to stop nursing and don't know how to do it.

Nighttime with Your Baby

Unless you are working from home, when you go back to work you are likely to see less of your baby. This can make two things happen. The first is that you miss your baby. That can make you feel sad or guilty. Or you may just want to spend as much time as you can with her when you're at home. The second thing that can happen is, you may be breastfeeding her less. Or you may be using a pump to express at work. This can also reduce the milk supply. Plenty of nursing when you are at home can help, and will also keep you close to your baby.

If your baby still wakes to nurse at night, you may want her to sleep in the same room with you. But make sure that your baby does not become overheated. The Foundation for the Study of Infant Deaths recommends that babies sleep in a bassinet or crib next to the parent's bed for at least the first six months. Even so, you can bring your baby into bed to nurse without having to get up. And you can rest while nursing her. Nighttime nursing can be tiring. You may have to work the next day. But it helps to know these night feedings will help maintain your milk supply.

Some parents still prefer to sleep with their babies in the same bed. Then you can nurse your baby and sleep at the same time. This way you keep up your milk supply and rest too. Some babies sleep better in bed with their parents, rather than alone in a crib. If the baby wakes, the breast is no

---

POSITIONING

Signs of a well-positioned baby

- Wide-open mouth
- Tongue underneath breast
- Bottom lip turned out
- Cheeks not drawn in
- Movement around temple or ears
- Mother not sore
- Baby's lower jaw taking good mouthful of areola
- Periods of fast and slow nursing

When you breastfeed, the baby's body must be in a straight line. Then she won't have to turn her neck or her body to reach the breast. As long as this is the case, you can feed her in any position.

more than a turn away. You don't have to go get the baby and settle her down again later. And you end up spending more time together.

Expressing Milk

The good thing about this system is that you can give your baby breast milk even when you are at work. You know that your baby still receives the best nutrition when you are away. When you express your milk, other people can feed the baby from a bottle or from a cup.

Expressing milk means you remove milk from the breast without the baby's help. There are a number of ways to do this:

- Express by hand

- Express by hand-held pump

- Express by battery-operated pump

- Express by electric pump

Distasteful?

Some people just don't like the idea of expressing. It makes them feel like a cow. Or they don't like to handle their own breasts. There are also different types of pumps. Some women prefer to express by hand. They feel being attached to a pump is, somehow, not quite right. Others find that machines work best.

No matter the method, pumping takes time. Some women can express eight ounces at the drop of a hat. But for most of us, this is a skill to learn. It takes patience and sometimes privacy. And, of course, you have to stick with it. If you want to succeed at expressing milk, keep at it.

What If You Don't Want to Express?

You hear that breastfeeding is best for the baby, that it gets easier and so on. But what if you don't want to? Some mothers feel pressure to breastfeed. Maybe their partner feels strongly in favor of it. Maybe everyone in their peer group breastfeeds.

Sometimes going back to work is enough to deal with, without the added pressure of "Should I or shouldn't I pump?" If you feel this way, you may feel better if you just do what feels right for you and your family.

Laura didn't express milk. But she kept nursing at night and each morning. *"I didn't express because my baby was six months old by the time I went back to work. I didn't think I needed to. She was old enough to take other foods besides breast milk."*

Your Flexible Friend

If you do want to continue to breastfeed, one of the benefits is that it's flexible. You can nurse as much or as little as you want. For instance, you can nurse just mornings and nights. That way, there's no need to express. Or you can completely breastfeed your baby if you express during the day when you are at work.

Often babies like to be fed at night. If you choose to nurse mornings and nights only, a long nighttime feeding can help you spend more time with your baby. It will also help you keep up your milk supply.

Supply and demand is at work here. The more your baby nurses, the more milk you make. Likewise, the less your baby nurses, the less milk you make. So if you want to feed twice daily, your body will adapt. And you should be able to supply your baby with her needs.

Pumps and Things

There are two ways to breastfeed. One requires no more than a nursing mother and her baby. The other is more high-tech. It can involve electric pumps that cost hundreds of dollars, travel bags, storage bags, bottles . . . the list is endless. At least we now have the choice to make breastfeeding what we want it to be! We can choose long-distance breastfeeding while we are at work. We now have the methods to make it possible.

The cheapest way to express milk is by hand. Even so, you will need equipment to store it in, collect it in, and maybe freeze it in. Hand expression works by massaging the breast with the hand. It is very effective for some. It's also worth knowing how to do. You can hand express to relieve engorgement if you ever need to.

As pumps get more complicated, the price goes up. More expensive pumps don't always work better. One type of hand pump requires two hands to operate. There's also a hand pump you can use with one hand. There are battery pumps and electric pumps that convert to hand pumps. And there are the large electric pumps that are used in hospitals. You can often rent them for short-term use.

Some mothers like to build up a good supply of milk to keep in the freezer before they go back to work. This removes the pressure to express each day for the next day, because on some days you may not have the time. A mother could express after nursing once a day for maybe a month before going back to work. Or she could express after one feeding for two weeks and after two feedings for the next two weeks. It partly depends on how often you will be able to express once you are back in the office. If once a day is the maximum, it may be best to leave it at that. Then your body won't have to adjust to the decrease in demand when you work.

Don't be concerned by the amount of milk you express at first. There are tricks that may help. These are mentioned later in this chapter. But you have to be able to relax. You must also believe that you can do it.

GUIDELINES

Guidelines for Expressing

- When you express milk, you will make more milk. If you are building up a supply before going back to work, look out for signs of engorgement.

- If you plan to nurse just mornings and nights, give your body time to adjust to the new pattern. Drop feedings slowly, say one every other day. Then you shouldn't feel any discomfort. If you do feel full in the middle of the day, you could express enough to relieve the discomfort.

- Try to make changes *after* your milk supply is established, not before. This often takes four to six weeks after birth.

- Try to make any changes well before you return to work. Then you won't be sitting at a desk with rock-hard breasts, aching to release the milk.

- Your hormones may not respond as well to a pump as to the baby nursing. This could make your supply begin to taper off. You can solve this by nursing the baby more often during the weekend. Or you could extend evening feedings.

- Think about the method you want to use well in advance. Pumps aren't cheap. It's expensive to keep buying different ones to try them out. Maybe you know people whose pump you could borrow. A La Leche League leader may have a pump you could try. Or you could start with the cheapest method and work up from there.

- There is a risk that the baby will begin to prefer the bottle. This happens sometimes. Think about how you would feel if your baby chose the time of her weaning.

Choosing Your Method

This is a question of what you prefer. The next few pages will help you decide. You could spend hundreds of dollars finding a method that suits you. You might buy all the gadgets "that every working mother can't do without," as the ads tell you.

Many people will find that they can express by all methods. Others find only one suits them. But you can find ways to express that give your body a chance to get the milk flowing.

Making Expressing Work

Relax is the key word. Easier said than done? Maybe! But once you start, it will get easier all the time.

Some people find being alone helps them to relax completely. Others prefer someone to talk to.

Remind yourself of how you learned to relax for labor. That will help you unwind now. Find a place where you feel at ease. If you are perched over a sink or sitting on the edge of a chair, you may not feel too calm. Practice clenching muscles and then slowly relaxing them. This may make you feel more fully relaxed.

Louisa had to express in a tough place. *"I found expressing at work nerve-wracking. Although I had my own examining room, I used to sit against the door and things like that. I used to say to myself, 'I need this milk.' And nothing would come out . . . or the pump would squeak."*

On the other hand, Lucy runs workshops. She would express in the classrooms during her lunchtime without any problems.

Warmth

Being warm helps breast milk to flow. Take a shower and just let the water flow over you for a few minutes before you express. Or lie in a bath. The warm water may help you relax at the same time. Lots of women find that soaking in a bath makes the milk start to flow. This can give you some comfort.

If you don't want to take a bath, try warm washcloths. Or wrap a hot-water bottle in a towel and lay it on your chest.

The Power of Positive Thinking

You need to get the let-down reflex working if you are to express. It responds to the baby's suckling. But it can also be triggered by thinking about the baby or hearing the baby. This can sometimes work against you. You might start to leak if you hear a baby crying, or someone at the office asks you about your baby. Or you'll feel a tingling in your breasts. If this happens to you, cross your arms. That will help stop the flow. Or push your hand against your breast. Of course, it can look a little strange to sit in a meeting, arms tightly crossed. But don't worry, the sensation passes in a few seconds.

Chrissy used a photo of her baby for her pumping sessions: *"I didn't find it easy to express. But I took a photo of Gary with me to work. That seemed to do the trick."*

Sometimes just thinking about the baby is enough to trigger the let-down.

You could, like Chrissy, take something that belongs to the baby with you. It could be a piece of clothing or a tape of her gurgling.

Hand Expressing

You will need something to express the milk into. It works best if the container is wide-rimmed. It will need to be sterile. Any other bottles you use will also need to be sterile.

Wash your hands before starting to express.

It is easy to damage the delicate tissue of the breast. Be sure you don't push too hard.

When you start to express, don't expect to be able to do it quickly. At first, it may take up to 45 minutes. The length of time will reduce with practice.

The Morning Feeding

One of the best times to express is after an early-morning feeding. Your body has rested all night. Nighttime is also when your body is best at making milk. You will often have more milk upon waking than your baby needs.

FEEDING FILE

Expressing Milk by Hand

The Good

- No special equipment is needed. You only need a wide-necked sterile container and clean hands.
- Hand expressing is closer to a baby's suckling action than using a pump. That's why it may be a better way to maintain the milk supply.
- Expressing by hand may be gentler than expressing with a pump.

The Bad

- It may take longer to express by hand than by pump.
- Your hands may get tired.

How to Hand Express

- Use a hand to cup your breast from underneath. Put your forefinger along the line where your areola and breast meet. Place your thumb on top of your breast, along the same line.
- Your milk is stored in pools just below this line. These pools need to be squeezed gently to extract the milk. You may need to move in your hand slightly, towards your nipple, or back, towards your chest, to find the pools of milk. Practice until you find the right place for you.
- Gently squeeze your thumb and fingers together. Push back and in towards your ribcage at the same time. This combined movement helps push the milk along the ducts toward the nipple. It also helps squeeze out the milk.
- Relax the pressure, then repeat the movement.
- Your milk may take a minute or two to flow. Don't give up if nothing happens right away!
- Move your hand around your breast. That way you can cover all the milk ducts. You could also change hands on the same breast.
- If your hand gets tired, change sides. Go back to the first side later.
- It might be easier to learn to express by hand after you have been shown how. Your midwife, breastfeeding counselor or La Leche League leader may be able to help you.
- The best way to learn may be to watch someone who is able to do it. Ask your breastfeeding counselor or La Leche League leader if she knows someone who might show you how.

Another way to build up a store of milk is to wait for an hour or so after a morning feeding. When your supplies have built up again, express as much as you can to store for later. Then your milk will build up for the next feeding.

Of course, there may be times when your baby will be hungry sooner than usual. The normal supply of milk may not be there. Or sometimes your baby may go longer between feedings. This can leave you full and anxious to get rid of the milk. Once you get into a routine, such problems lessen or disappear.

If you express right after one of your baby's feedings, your baby will have brought on the let-down reflex. You won't have to start "cold." You might also use a one-hand pump. Then you can feed the baby from one breast, and express from the other. This may take some practice. But it can work well.

The let-down doesn't only appear at the start of a feeding. It happens from time to time during a feeding, too. If you feel you have run out of milk when you express, you may find that by going a little longer, you'll get another surge of milk. But stop expressing if you start to get sore.

Hand Pumps

Again, the pump needs to be sterile. Fortunately, modern pumps are easy to take apart to sterilize.

Hand pumps are the cheapest type of pump. They are easy to move around and fairly quiet.

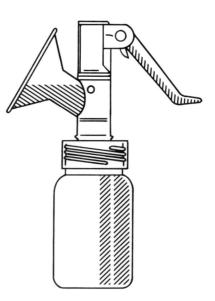

When Sarah went back to work she was happy with her hand pump: *"I used it at work twice a day, for about 15-20 minutes at a time. I was lucky. I worked in a hospital and could find places where I could express in peace. I used two sterilized bottles. I'd put them in the refrigerator. They were still cold when I got home."*

Battery Pumps

These pumps are more expensive. Some can be plugged in to a wall outlet. Battery pumps save your hand from getting worn out pumping. But you use a lot of batteries unless you get the kind you can recharge. These pumps can be noisier than a hand pump. Sometimes noise doesn't matter. But if you have to express in the bathroom at work, you may not want your colleagues wondering what you're doing.

Electric Pumps

These are large pumps. They are very heavy and expensive. These pumps are used in hospital neonatal intensive care units (NICU). You can rent one from some hospitals or through La Leche League. The newer models are coming out in pale, creamy shades. They used to be gunmetal gray and not too pretty!

Nearly all mothers are successful with this type of pump. These pumps are also good because you can do *dual pumping* with them. That means you can express from both breasts at the same time, which saves you time. The down side is, they are not portable. The rental fee can add up over time.

Electric pumps are mainly for mothers of babies in intensive care. Such mothers need to establish their milk supply without the baby's help. They are also used by mothers whose babies cannot nurse for any other reason. They would be useful to rent for a short time to build up a supply of milk before going back to work.

Vanessa is a pump agent for the Egnell Ameda company. That means she rents pumps to anyone who needs them. She has about six pumps. *"I'd say that most women who rent pumps use them to get breastfeeding started. Maybe their baby has been in intensive care and now they are home. Or they might need to build up their milk supply. A number of mothers use them to build up a store of milk before going back to work. Some mothers rent them because their baby is refusing the breast for some reason and they want to maintain their supply."*

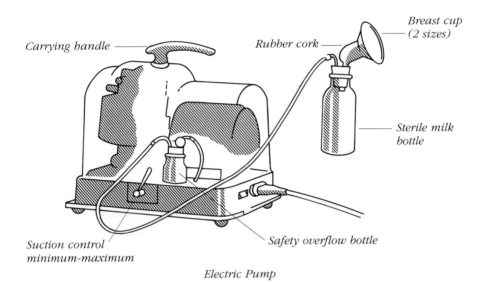

Carrying handle

Rubber cork

Breast cup
(2 sizes)

Sterile milk
bottle

Suction control
minimum-maximum

Safety overflow bottle

Electric Pump

A small version of the electric breast pump is available now. It is a hand pump with a motor attached. It can convert to a hand pump if needed. These pumps cost much less than the large hospital models.

Freezing

If you express a number of times a day, you can add milk to the same storage container. But you should cool the newly expressed milk first for 30 minutes in the refrigerator. After that, add it to milk you have already collected. At the end of the day, date and freeze the milk.

You can also add fresh milk to frozen milk. But add no more than 50% fresh milk to frozen. In other words, if you have 6 ounces in the freezer, do not add more than 3 ounces to it. Milk can be frozen for up to three months in a household freezer. It can be kept for seven days in the freezer compartment of a refrigerator. If you have added fresh milk to frozen milk, use it all up by the date that is right for the first milk.

Defrosting

One of the best ways to thaw breast milk is to hold the container under cold running water. Slowly add warmer water until the milk is thawed and warmed to room temperature.

Breast milk should not be heated in a microwave oven. Key substances in the milk will be destroyed if it gets too hot. Also, microwave ovens don't heat liquids evenly. Hot spots in the milk could burn the baby.

Babies and Bottles

This is an important section. Try as we might, some babies don't like to take the bottle. Breastfeeding requires a certain way of sucking. Bottle-feeding requires another way. If a baby starts to learn how to get milk from a bottle, she may want to keep on sucking that way. But some babies take to a bottle when offered one at three months and move back to the breast for the next feeding.

> ### STORAGE
>
> All containers that milk is expressed into must be sterile. All storage containers must be sterile, too. Make sure all the milk you store is dated. Fresh milk can be stored in the refrigerator for 24 hours. If the milk goes bad, it won't smell right.
>
> Storage containers:
>
> • Plastic bottles
>
> • Milk freezer bags. You can attach them to some pumps and express right into them. Some of them are *laminated*—they have a layer between the milk and the plastic.
>
> • Ice-cube trays are also good for freezing breast milk in.

The facts seem to be that babies get the hang of breastfeeding. Then they expect to get their milk that way. If breastfeeding is all they know for the first three months, they may find it hard to adjust to a bottle.

Does that mean that it isn't worth starting to breastfeed if you plan to return to work?

There are still plenty of reasons to breastfeed if you are working. But some mothers are sure to worry "will she or won't she take the bottle?"

When to Begin Offering the Bottle

It's good to offer a bottle early in the baby's life. If your baby gets used to a bottle it's simpler to go back to work, or have a night out. It's best to wait until breastfeeding is established before you offer a bottle. This way, the baby gets used to breastfeeding first. But some mothers prefer to offer the bottle sooner than that.

Amy, with four children, says: *"I didn't have any problems with my babies taking the bottle. I introduced one a week, with water in it, very early, in the first couple of weeks."*

TRANSPORTING MILK

If you plan to express at work, the milk has to get from your office to your baby. There is often a waiting period in between. These are some factors you need to think about:

Distance

If you live an hour from your office, you will need a more elaborate cooler system than for a short drive. A thermal bag with a cool pack in it would only suffice for a five-minute walk, for example.

Time of year

On hot days, breast milk will sour more quickly. You will need to pay more attention to it in warm weather.

Method of transport

If you put a bottle of breast milk on the back seat of your own car, it's not the same as putting it on the seat beside you on a commuter train—where people *will* notice it. A sign that says, "Jill's breast milk—DO NOT DRINK" might be useful while it is in the refrigerator at work. But some people don't like the thought of breast milk except in you or the baby. (Some people don't even like that!) You know it's *their* problem. But they may make you feel awkward about it.

Office conditions

Maybe your office is well-equipped. You can store your expressed breast milk (EBM) in a refrigerator. But many offices don't have a good refrigerator. Or if there is one, it may be three floors away and not worth the trip. This is something to think about. Either march to the refrigerator twice a day, or make sure your own cooler system is as effective as possible.

Breast milk needs to be kept chilled, to reduce the risk of growing germs. There are now travel bags made just for working mothers who express at work. They aren't essential, however. Lots of people have their own methods of transport, like Julie: *"I expressed at work. But I didn't want anyone to know what I was doing. It's not a mother-friendly office. So I did it in the ladies lounge. I used to store the milk in plastic cottage-cheese containers and put it in the refrigerator. No one ever found out . . . as far as I know."*

Louisa: *"I gave a bottle of expressed breast milk in the first week or so to my first baby. It worked. I did it with the others, who didn't have a problem taking a bottle, either."*

It's possible the baby will come to prefer the bottle to the breast. Milk comes out more quickly from a bottle, and the baby may like that. There is no waiting around for the let-down. Older babies may prefer the better view they get while bottle-feeding. Rather than being snuggled into their mother's breast, they can look at the outside world.

Sue found that her daughter's interest changed. *"It was cuddly, nice for her and nice for me. It was really the best thing for her. But in the end she got used to the bottle and getting the milk more quickly."*

Getting Your Baby to Try the Bottle

Nothing works all the time. Patience, persistence and time all help. Your baby is not being naughty if she shows no interest in a bottle at first. She doesn't know what she is being offered. (Imagine what it might feel like if someone tried to push a tube of toothpaste in your mouth!) Try to let her explore the nipple. Don't force it into her mouth. Here are some things mothers have tried:

- Her mother is the person least likely to succeed in bottle-feeding her at first. See if your partner or a friend will try when you are out of the room.

- At first, don't put her in her normal nursing position. That will make her expect the breast.

- Warm the nipple of the bottle slightly, so it is more pliable.

- Squeeze some breast milk onto her lips from the bottle.

- Offer her the breast first. Then give her the bottle when she is relaxed and not starving.

- Offer her the bottle in a dark room. Try this when she has woken up and is relaxed.

- Give her lots of cuddling and tenderness when offering the bottle. Then she won't miss out on the closeness of breastfeeding.

• If she won't take milk from a bottle, try a cup or a spoon.

If your baby won't take the bottle, you may feel upset. A mother can feel awful at the thought of not only leaving her baby, but leaving her to "starve" because she won't take a bottle. If this happens to you, think of ways around it. If your baby is old enough, you may be able to offer the milk in other forms. You can mix the milk with baby rice or other first foods. At least in this way you know your baby is getting her nourishment.

Sandy went back to work part-time when her daughter was five months old. *"I was at work for two long days. I would express at work at lunch time. I'd breastfed her before I left. I offered her a bottle, a spout, a spoon and a cup. She didn't take any of them. But there was no use going crazy about it. The age factor had a lot to do with how I coped. If she had been two and a half months, it would have been much harder."*

Kerry also had problems with a bottle. *"I tried a bottle when she was about four months old. She had used them when she was a tiny baby. We thought it would be OK. But no way, not from anyone. After a while, we tried with a cup. Since she was a big baby, that was OK. So I kept on nursing her morning and night. During the day she had formula from a cup. That way she didn't have to give up nursing after I went back to work. That was good, too. I'd do the same thing again."*

Often mothers are told, "Don't worry, your baby won't starve herself." This is true. But does it help to know that? It may be better to think, "If she won't take a bottle today, maybe she will tomorrow, or the next day." And if she still doesn't take it, you can try other things. A battle at each feeding time won't help either baby or parent.

Breastfeeding and the Working Mother

Some people think that while breastfeeding is fine, the activity is best kept in the home. These people think nursing doesn't fit with being a working mother. But people who think otherwise are speaking up. They insist that being a working mother doesn't mean you have to deny you have a family all day long.

Both breastfeeding and working can have their limits. For instance, some mothers do not feel they can admit that they express at work.

Heather: *"I worked for an accounting firm. It was awful. I thought I'd lose the respect of my subordinates, if they knew what I was doing."*

Then there can be problems with the office "uniform," as Louisa found. *"The main problem I had going back to work early was my waistline. I had nothing to wear. None of my prepregnancy clothes fit. And since I expressed at lunch times, I couldn't wear a dress. I would have had to strip to express the milk."*

Then there are the times your breasts leak. Fortunately there are ways around this. Alex went back to work when her second baby was 14 weeks old. *"To prevent leaks from showing, I always made sure I had a sweater or a jacket close by. Also I treated myself to some nice bras, so I wouldn't feel so milky. I bought some camisole tops, too. Then my nursing bras didn't show through my blouse."*

You also might want to invest in extra shirts or blouses. Keep a few at the office in case you leak a lot. Stains show less on dark and patterned fabric. A spare box of breast pads in the office is useful too. Good breast pads can make you feel more secure about leaks.

If you don't express during the day, or if you have to work late, you can get so full your breasts hurt. Sally works in the medical field. *"When I first went back to work, I would leak through my surgical outfit. But my body adapted in a week or so. My colleagues were very supportive. And I had my own office where I could express. But if I had a late operation, followed by office appointments, then the pressure would build."*

Sometimes when women return to work, they change their clothes and their hair. Maybe they start to wear perfume again. This sort of thing can affect the baby. Louisa suggests that *"You should put on perfume as soon as you have your baby. If you don't, once you get back to work and start wearing it again, your baby may react to it and refuse the breast. Besides, perfume makes you feel better."*

Alex rented a pump for four months. She used it daily. But her baby refused the bottle each time. So Alex mixed the milk in her baby's food. And her baby would take juice from a bottle. In time she tried a formula milk that her baby liked. Then breastfeeding came to an end.

These are just some of the things you may think about.

- Do you want to express at work or just nurse at home?

- How long will it take you to express in the office?

- Does your office have a room where you can express in private?

- Will time spent expressing come out of your lunch hour, or will it be extra?

- Do you want people to know? How will you feel if they do know?

LOOK OUT FOR:

- Engorged breasts, while you adjust to a new nursing schedule.
- Blocked ducts. This can happen when you commute and are cramped or have to sit in one position.
- Mastitis can be an inflamed or infected breast. It can be caused when blocked ducts or engorgement are not taken care of. Mastitis can make you feel awful, with flu-like symptoms.

ANSWERS

Answers for these problems can be any of the following:

- Don't drop feedings too quickly. You may become engorged.
- If you do feel too full at work, express a little milk until you feel better.
- Try not to lock your body in one position at work, such as sitting before a computer screen. Walk around the office every half-hour or so.
- If you do get engorged, do what you can to feel better in the office. Then go home and nurse your baby for a good long time. You can also take a long bath and express into the bath until you feel better.
- Make sure all your bras fit well. Don't ever wear a bra to bed at night.
- Look after yourself. Try to keep up your energy with frequent, healthy snacks. Rest as much as you can after work.

Problems with Breastfeeding and Working

Most problems come about because the milk is not coming out of the breast well. The baby's position may be poor, so she can't remove the milk as she should.

Other factors about working can cause problems.

Nothing is worse than getting mastitis as you set out to become a working mother. Always think about how much you are doing, and how much rest you can get. Eat well. Stay away from the office diet of coffee all day long. Move around frequently. This will help you keep up your milk supply. And you'll work better, too.

It takes more effort to breastfeed when you are back at work. But it can be very rewarding if you want to do it.

Worth the Extra Effort

Breastfeeding mothers who return to work often find their nursing to be a good thing. They get the fulfillment of being at work and being a wage earner. They also maximize their babies' nutrition. The babies continue to receive immune factors through the breast milk, which help protect them against illness.

Michele went back to work when her baby was three months old. *"Although I was ready to start working again, I felt Suzanne could still benefit from breastfeeding. I could express milk at work, so the situation worked for us. Work was interesting for me—I wanted to be there. I knew she was getting the best food. It took some time and I had to be organized. But I'm glad I did it. Once I got the hang of expressing milk, the whole process became quick and easy. I really think it's worth making the extra effort. Certainly it is worth it if you are going back to work when your baby is very young."*

Conclusion

Finding the Balance

"A balancing act," "a juggling act," "never any time to yourself." These comments are common in the world of working parents. It can be quite a challenge to resolve all the needs of a family and to enjoy a role in the workplace.

Your work can give you a sense of purpose and completeness that you may not get without it. For many parents, raising children is their whole world. *"I feel I have the best of both worlds in my life at the moment. I love my children. And I love being with them. But that isn't the same as loving being sole caregiver for 12 to 13 hours a day. Having a job means I can do something for myself and then come home, happy and not at the end of my rope by afternoon. I think that full-time mothering can be very lonely. I need to focus on more than just my children. I think it will make me more interesting to them. I also want them to have a female role model who works as well as cares for them."*

If you are thinking of going back to work, you have to find the balance that is right for you. Your life can be enriched by your work if it is within your own boundaries and limits. This may be a couple of hours a week, or full-time. Finding out what will suit you is an essential part of the process. To do so you must look at the options that are open to you. Each person is different. What suits one person may not work for another. You cannot pretend you only have yourself to please after having a family. But you do need to look after your own needs. Think about what matters to you. Then see how this can be embraced along with the needs of others in your life.

This is a good time to take a look at the many workstyles from which you can choose. You have part-time, full-time or flex-time as options. You can also work from home more often these days. Think about your choices. The working world today is no longer so "all or nothing." Women are likely to continue to want children. But it is not so easy to replace them at work. Their status and duties have risen to a greater extent than ever before. This means that more employers will be prepared to listen to you. They will give greater attention to the needs of working parents.

As Laura says: *"It's all about balance. If you can get it right, you can look forward to a very fulfilling lifestyle, enriched by what matters most to you."*

Resources

Here are the names and addresses of useful groups and information to give you a better idea of their purpose.

American Council of Nanny Schools, phone (517) 686-9417. This nonprofit agency oversees the training of nannies. It can refer parents to one of its nanny schools.

Battered Women's Justice Project, phone 1-800-903-0111; fax (612) 824-8965.

Business Solutions, St. Paul Pioneer Press, 345 Cedar St., St. Paul, MN 55101, phone (612) 222-2857; fax (612) 222-6129. Business Solutions uses a group of experts to provide ideas and answers to business problems.

Canadian Child Care Federation, phone (613) 729-5289.

Child Care Action Campaign, 330 Seventh Ave., 17th floor, New York, NY 10001-5010. Send a self-addressed, stamped envelope to receive a free copy of "Finding and Hiring a Qualified In-Home Caregiver." Ask for Information Guide 20.

Child Care Aware, phone 1-800-424-2246.

Danny Foundation, 3158 Danville Blvd., P.O. Box 680, Alamo, CA 94507. Phone 1-800-DANNY. The Danny Foundation provides information on the dangers of cribs.

Depression After Delivery, P.O. Box 1282, Morrisville, PA 19067. Phone 1-800-944-4773 to leave a message.

Doulas of North America (DONA), 1100 23rd Ave. East, Seattle, WA 98112. Phone (206) 324-5440; fax (206) 325-0472; Internet AskDONA@aol.com http://www.dona.com/ DONA trains and certifies doulas. It also refers pregnant women to certified doulas.

Internal Revenue Service (IRS) phone 1-800-829-1040. Call to learn how childcare expenses affect your taxes.

La Leche League, 1400 North Meacham Rd., Schaumburg, IL 60173-4840. Phone 1-800-LA-LECHE, or (708) 519-7730. La Leche League provides free information and support for breastfeeding mothers. You may be referred to a trained leader in your area.

Medela, Inc., P.O. Box 660, McHenry, IL 60051. Phone 1-800-TELL-YOU. Medela makes effective breast pumps for mothers who want to express their breast milk.

Mothers At Home, phone 1-800-783-4666. Support for mothers who may be planning to leave the workplace. Free newsletter, "Welcome Home."

National Association of Child Care Resource and Referral Agencies, Washington, D.C. (202) 393-5501. Resource and referral agencies help parents find child care. They also provide training for childcare workers and can help them solve the problems they face.

National Child Abuse Hotline, phone 1-800-4A-CHILD (1-800-422-4453).

National Child Care Information Center, 301 Maple Ave. West, Suite 602, Vienna, VA 22180. Phone 1-800-616-2242; fax 1-800-716-2242. The Center provides childcare information to states, territories and tribes, policy makers, parents, programs and the public. Its Child Care Bulletin is published six times a year.

National Coalition Against Domestic Violence, P.O. Box 18749, Denver, CO 80218. Phone (303) 839-1852; fax (303) 831-9251.

National Committee to Prevent Child Abuse, 332 S. Michigan Ave., Chicago, IL 60604. Phone (312) 663-3520; fax (312) 939-8962.

National Council on Child Abuse and Family Violence, 1155 Connecticut Ave., NW, Suite 400, Washington, D.C. 20036. Phone (202) 429-6695 or 1-800-222-2000

National Domestic Violence Hotline, 1-800-799-SAFE (7233); TDD number for the hearing impaired is 1-800-787-3224.

National Organization of Single Mothers, P.O. Box 68, Midland, NC 28107-0068. Phone (704) 888-KIDS.

Parents Anonymous Hotline, phone 1-800-421-0353. In California, 1-800-352-0368.

Parenting magazine, phone (303) 682-8878 to subscribe.

Parents magazine, P.O. Box 3042, Harlan, IA 51537-0207. Phone 1-800-727-3682.

Resource Center on Child Protection and Custody, phone 1-800-527-3223; fax (702) 784-6160.

Trustline Registry, phone 1-800-822-8490. Located in California. Provides free background checks for unlicensed childcare workers.

Unions: If your company is unionized, you can make use of this to ensure you get fair treatment, as an employee, as a woman and as a parent. Unions will offer to help you negotiate for childcare assistance, career breaks or job shares. If you have a union you may find that policies are already in place. But your union will often help you get the best deal.

For example, a career-break structure introduced by one union represents good practice. The basic points of this plan are:

- It is open to both men and women. Workers can apply and reach a decision before starting a family.

- Two periods of leave are possible, for a maximum of two years each. These can be full- or part-time.

- Employee's and employer's contributions to the pension plan can be maintained.

- Flexible or part-time return is possible.

- Return to same grade at same or nearby location.

United States Information Agency (USIA), phone (202) 619-4355. USIA will provide referral to the eight au pair agencies, which they oversee.

Wellstart, 4062 First Ave., San Diego, CA 92103. Phone (619) 295-5192. Wellstart provides information about breastfeeding. It also trains healthcare providers from all over the world about breastfeeding.

Women's Bureau, United States Department of Labor, Women's Bureau Clearing House, Box EX, 200 Constitution Ave., NW, Washington, D.C. 20210. Phone 1-800-827-5335. The Women's Bureau can provide information about state laws on family leave.

Working Mother magazine, 135 West 50th St., New York, NY 10020.

Index

Other helpful books in this series

$12.95 pb • ISBN 1-55561-122-2
$17.95 Canada
6 x 9, 234 pages

Breastfeeding Your Baby
A National Childbirth Trust Guide

Jane Moody, Jane Britten and Karen Hogg

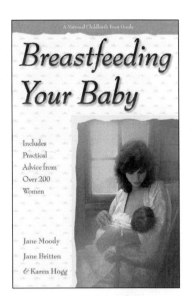

Reassuring, comprehensive advice on a subject of increasing interest to a new generation of mothers.

How does breastfeeding work? How do mothers breastfeed premature babies?

What's special about breast milk? Can you breastfeed twins? Will I enjoy breastfeeding?

Over 200 mothers describe what helps and what hinders the breastfeeding experience. Written by three breastfeeding counselors, this up-to-date book answers the variety of questions parents have about breastfeeding, so they can decide what's right for *them.*

$12.95 pb • ISBN 1-55561-125-7
$17.95 Canada
6 x 9, 254 pages, b/w illustrations

Your Newborn and You
A National Childbirth Trust Guide

Anna McGrail

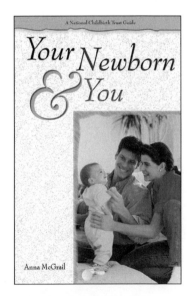

What will being a parent really be like? How will I cope with the basics, such as changing diapers? What's the best way to ensure a good night's sleep? How will we manage the change in our lives? Will sex ever be the same again?

Parenting is a hands-on skill—you learn as you go, but you can pick up most from the real experts: other parents. While there is often no right or wrong way to handle things, the suggestions and experiences of other mothers and fathers can help you decide what is right for you and your child.

.ll also enjoy our most popular "Your Pregnancy" series

$12.95 pb • ISBN 1-55561-143-5
$17.95 Canada
6.125 x 9.25, 384 pages, b/w illustrations throughout

Your Pregnancy Week by Week
Third Edition
Glade B. Curtis, MD, OB/GYN

Completely updated in its third edition, *Your Pregnancy Week by Week* is the top-selling pregnancy book written by a doctor.

Dr. Curtis designed its unique format to help all women from before they conceive their baby until they give birth.

$12.95 pb • 1-55561-150-8
$17.95 Canada
6.125 x 9.25, 448 pages, illustrated

Your Pregnancy Questions & Answers
Glade B. Curtis, MD, OB/GYN

This bestseller is in an easy-to-read question-and-answer format. In Dr. Curtis' warm style, he thoughtfully answers over 1,200 questions pregnant women ask most often.

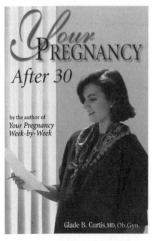

$12.95 pb • 1-55561-088-9
$17.95 Canada
6.125 x 9.25, 384 pages, illustrated

Your Pregnancy After 30
Glade B. Curtis, MD, OB/GYN

The latest in this best-selling series—an important and timely resource for the rapidly growing number of women becoming pregnant after age 30.